Better Homes and Gardens®
1991
DECORATING
& REMODELING

© Copyright 1991 by Meredith Corporation, Des Moines, Iowa.
All Rights Reserved. Printed in the United States of America.
First Edition. First Printing.
ISSN: 1046-459X
ISBN: 0-696-01921-3

Better Homes and Gardens®

Editor DAVID JORDAN
Managing Editor LAMONT OLSON
Art Director BRADFORD W.S. HONG

Interior Design
Editor DENISE L. CARINGER
Interior Design Editor ROBERT E. DITTMER
Senior Interior Design Editor SANDRA S. SORIA
Senior Crafts and Tabletop Editor JILANN SEVERSON
Associate Editor REBECCA JERDEE
Editorial Assistant SUSAN McBROOM

Graphic Design
Associate Art Directors
PAUL ZIMMERMAN   TIM ALEXANDER
Cover Designer NANCY KLUENDER
Senior Graphic Designer DAN BISHOP
Graphic Designers KELLY BARTON
KEVIN S. LUDGATE   SUSAN LYNN UEDELHOFEN
Design Assistant CHRISTY HAND

Building and Remodeling
Editor JOAN McCLOSKEY
Senior Building and Remodeling Editor WILLIAM L. NOLAN
Building and Environmental Editor TOM JACKSON
Associate Editor SUSAN SOUDER
Editorial Assistant MARILYN SCOTT

Copy and Production
Copy Chief ELIZABETH HAHN BROOKS
Makeup Editor LINDA R. THOMAS
Associate Makeup Editor CINDY L. ALBERTS
Electronic Text Facilitator NANCY HALL
Electronic Design Facilitator MICKIE VORHES
Administrative Assistant GINGER BASSETT
Editorial Assistant DIANA PRENDERGAST

Editorial Marketing Services
Director MARGARET McMAHON
Mail Order Shopping Editor ARLENE AVILES

Editorial Services
Manager of Editorial Services and Planning DAVID S. JOHNSON
Supervisor of Editorial Administrative Services ROSE ANDERSON
Art Business Office Manager DIANE BOYLE   *Photo Studio Manager* DON WIPPERMAN

Editorial Research
Director C. RAY DEATON   *Research Assistant* SCOTT R. TOLAN

Group Vice President *Editorial Director* **DORIS M. EBY**
Creative Director, Product Development DAVID R. HAUPERT
Public Relations CYNTHIA ADAMS

Senior Vice President/Publishing Director, Better Homes and Gardens
ADOLPH AUERBACHER
Publisher JERRY KAPLAN
Business Manager TERRY UNSWORTH   *Advertising Sales Director* ROBERT M. BAXTER
Research Director HUGH CURLEY   *Director of Sales Promotion and Merchandising* JOANNA DALES
Production Director ROBERT C. FURSTENAU

MAGAZINE GROUP PRESIDENT JAMES A. AUTRY
Magazine Group Vice Presidents Publishing Directors **ADOLPH AUERBACHER,**
BURTON H. BOERSMA, CHRISTOPHER M. LEHMAN, MYRNA BLYTH
DEAN PIETERS, Operations **MAX RUNCIMAN,** Finance

BETTER HOMES AND GARDENS® BOOKS
Editor GERALD M. KNOX
Art Director ERNEST SHELTON   Managing Editor: DAVID A. KIRCHNER

President, Book Group JERAMY LANDAUER
Vice President, Retail Marketing JAMIE L. MARTIN
Vice President, Administrative Services RICK RUNDALL

MEREDITH CORPORATION
CORPORATE OFFICERS: Chairman of the Executive Committee   E. T. MEREDITH III
Chairman of the Board ROBERT A. BURNETT
President and Chief Executive Officer JACK D. REHM
Group Presidents: JAMES A. AUTRY, Magazines
JERAMY LANDAUER, Books   W. C. McREYNOLDS, Broadcasting   ALLEN L. SABBAG, Real Estate
Vice Presidents: LEO R. ARMATIS, Corporate Relations   THOMAS G. FISHER, General Counsel and Secretary
JAMES F. STACK, Finance
Treasurer MICHAEL A. SELL   Corporate Controller and Assistant Secretary LARRY D. HARTSOOK

1991 DECORATING AND REMODELING
Editors: Denise L. Caringer and Joan McCloskey
Project Editor: Marsha Jahns
Assistant Art Director: Harijs Priekulis
Electronic Text Publishing: Paula Forest

CONTENTS

For more than 60 years, *Better Homes and Gardens*® magazine has been providing you with inspiration, ideas, and practical information on decorating and remodeling your home. Here, in *1991 Decorating and Remodeling*, we bring you a permanent collection of the best decorating and remodeling features that appeared in the pages of that magazine during 1990.

JANUARY

Better Homes and Gardens
DESIGNS FOR BUTTERICK

SLIP-COVER CHIC

SEW-IT-YOURSELF DECORATING

You can't tell this seating group by its cover. With fresh fabric, Butterick slipcover patterns, and a bit of stitchery, these everyday furnishings went to the top of the best-dressed list wearing two of the hottest looks in home fashion today. In need of a change of scenery at your place? Give your furniture the slip!

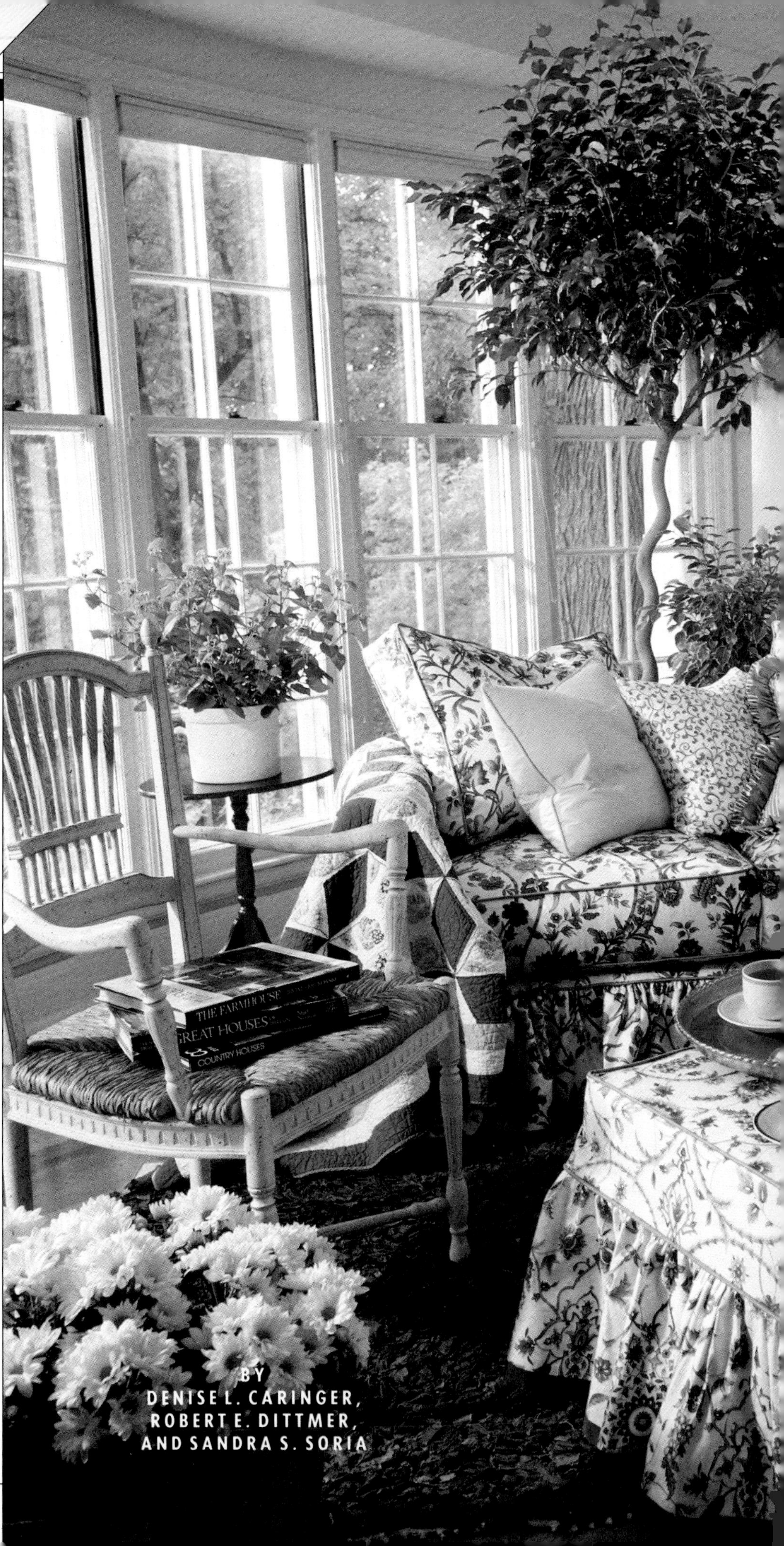

BY
DENISE L. CARINGER,
ROBERT E. DITTMER,
AND SANDRA S. SORIA

BEFORE. Slipcovers make fashion leaders from basic seaters.

A FRENCH ACCENT

Flouncy skirts and fabric as delicate as fine porcelain "romance" this setting with chic Provençal panache. Plump pillows cozy up the space while jolts of yellow warm up the cool blue-and-white palette. Pick up the slipcover and pillow pattern packages at the fabric store, and you'll have the savoir faire to outfit your furniture in the latest styles.

Slipcover pattern: No. 4592
Pillow pattern: No. 4593

GOTHIC ROMANCE

Look what a difference a change of fabric and frill can make! Tapestry tones and fancy finishing touches. give this room Gothic good looks, taking the same modern seating pieces back through centuries of style. The regal layering of patterns and shapely, well-dressed jumble of pillows create today's coveted opulent look.

You can tailor the slipcover to keep up with changes in furniture fashion—or changes in your mood! Sew more than one slipcover so you can make a quick wardrobe switch.

Slipcover pattern: No. 4592
Pillow pattern: No. 4593

STYLE STATEMENTS

Want to take your rooms from ho-hum to the height of fashion? Pay attention to detail! Sew-it-yourself style means you control the extras that tailor a look to your taste. Here's what makes the difference in our rooms.

PILLOWS TALK

When it comes to expressing today's styles, pillows are the punctuation mark. Dressed in a fresh mix of fabrics and given a touch of frill, these easy-to-sew toss pillows add some punch to a French country setting.

VS.

ALL THE TRIMMINGS

For a more opulent option, finish your pillows with a flourish. Stitch on some elegant extras, including ribbon, tassels, cord, or fringe, to give your seating pieces the royal treatment.

ACCENTS ON STYLE

Like characters who enter and exit scenes in a play, a room's accessories can be rotated to add fresh drama to a setting. Here, a delicate armchair, comforting quilt, and tub of sunny blooms speak with a decidedly French accent.

VS.

ENGLISH SUBJECTS

Switch a few supporting players and you have the makings of a whole new scene. The Gothic style is marked by hardy forms but graceful lines, such as those found in this chunky antique chair, stout topiary, and sturdy pedestal.

FOR THE FRILL OF IT

Although a soft element, fabric can be a strong character builder. The beauty of sew-it-yourself slipcovers is that you pick the fabric, then patterns help you decide what finishing touches you'll sew on, such as a ruffled skirt.

VS.

TAILORED AND TRIM

Trade in the light and airy fabric for one rich with tapestry tones and patterns, and you'll give the same piece an old outlook. Then, go for baroque with rich golden fringe.

ADDING ON A ROOM FOR COMFORT

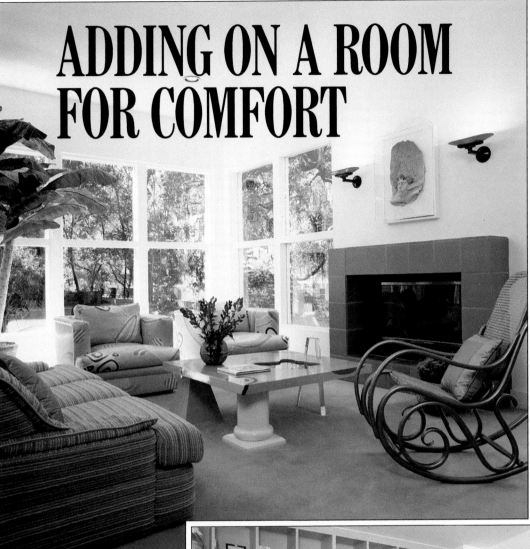

Conversation flows easily around the kid-conscious furnishings in this family gathering spot. The curved metal rocker wears a tough coat of auto paint.

The ash cabinetry in the wet bar matches the wood in the custom-built media wall. Grab a cold drink and sink in for some tube time.

Escape to this simple, sophisticated family room and view videos or vistas with your feet up and your hair down.

This tranquil blue oasis has all the creature comforts close at hand. Big, square, fixed windows wrap around one wall, changing the room's mood as the sun passes through. A soothing fire in the granite-fronted fireplace and soft uplighting beckon you to sink into a plush seat and unfurrow your brow.

The media wall nests the TV between closed-door compartments that tuck away other entertainment electronics. Orderly cubes above the cabinets turn everyday items and family memorabilia into an artistic display. The adjacent wet bar keeps snacks and beverages just steps away.

INTERIOR DESIGN: WENDY MARCUS GOER, ASID. REGIONAL EDITOR: RUTH L. REITER PHOTOGRAPHS: MIKE MORELAND. ARCHITECT: ROBERT EPPS, AIA

A '50s Ranch,
'90s Style

BY DENISE L. CARINGER
AND ROBERT E. DITTMER

Drowning in brown, this place could barely see the light.

Once running on empty, this room is cruisin' at top speed again. The fuel? White paint and fresh furnishings. Tune up your dated decor with these tactics:

- **Refuel with high-test white paint.**
- **Restore the interior with new miniblinds and oak flooring.**
- **Get more mileage per square foot with a fresh furniture arrangement.**

Ready to roll for the '90s, thanks to fresh paint, blinds, and flooring, this room gets comfort from cushy chairs and spice from southwestern accents.

A '50s Ranch, '90s Style

When Harry Wilk wanted to trade his sluggish decor for a sleeker "model," he asked us for help. Willing to start from scratch, Harry had no idea how to begin. Our advice? First, unify the background with white paint and ultra-slim "micro-mini" blinds. Next, install slick-but-warm oak floorboards, saving money with the do-it-yourself kind. Third, cozy up to the fireplace with leather-and-vinyl upholstery. An auto lover, Harry says, "This is great! With those chairs, the room smells like a new car."

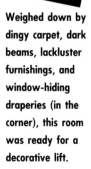

BEFORE

Moved from the dark dining L into the light, the old trestle table gets an updated look with country-chic chairs.

Weighed down by dingy carpet, dark beams, lackluster furnishings, and window-hiding draperies (in the corner), this room was ready for a decorative lift.

Special options—
rich rugs,
a desert-inspired
table, and colorful
accents (some
with a low "sticker
price")—make a
good room great.

A '50s Ranch, '90s Style

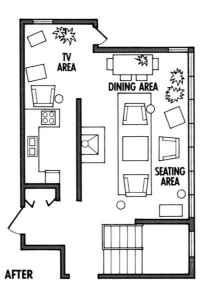

BEFORE
The dining L seemed dark and cramped.

The L makes a snug after-hours parking spot. Maneuverable, the chairs, TV, and ottomans "drive" around as needed.

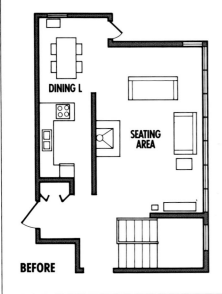

DINING L

SEATING AREA

BEFORE

TV AREA

DINING AREA

SEATING AREA

AFTER

To get better mileage per square foot, use old spaces in more efficient ways. Harry wanted a brighter dining spot and, if possible, a den, too. Solution? First, give the dining pieces a sunny outlook by the living room windows. Then, turn the dining L into a rest area for downshifting after a day in the fast lane. ▦

ENCHANTING ENTRIES

PERSONAL GREETINGS WELCOME WARMLY

BY SHARON N. O'KEEFE

Spotlighting the natural and the artful, this entry sets a serene mood.

A creative cluster of favorite pieces tells about this owner's life and loves.

Just beyond your home's threshold awaits the chance to make a memorable first impression. Coax your guests inside with a peek at your personal style.

PERSONAL PRELUDE

The contemporary entryway (*above left*) heralds the serene mood of living spaces beyond. From its sweep of hardwood flooring to the slick marble top on the antique French pastry table, an interplay of natural textures enlivens the white-on-white scheme. The paper collage introduces a blush of color, and the table's graceful underpinnings give the mix sculptural appeal. No wonder guests linger for a look. Aboard the table rests a child's clay rendition of Moby Dick—one that won its creator a coveted "A" on a school report.

GALLERY APPEAL

Visitors have come to expect the unexpected when they step into the sunwashed foyer (*above right*); its intriguing mix of art and artifacts changes at the whim of the collector-in-residence. The treasures she exhibits give the small entry special-space status and reveal her passions. Today, two leggy tables, a couple of stars from her cache of old-and-new pottery, striking black-and-white photographs, and a delicate lamp compose a telling vignette. Tomorrow, the tables, carrying new cargo, might be angled in a new way. The gallerylike backdrop is perfect for display, and an Oriental rug adds a warm touch to the cool tile floor.

USHER-IN STYLE

How does your entry introduce you?
● **Paint** a self-portrait with an upfront display of personal prizes. If you fancy vintage baskets, cluster them in an aged cupboard. Or, show off the family artist's skill in an entry grouping.
● **Link** your entry to the style of your home. If bold color sparks your living spaces, don't let the entry pale by comparison. Likewise, if your home is in a Victorian mood, don't leave the entry stranded in a modern-day time warp.
● **Think** smart about entry design. The scale of the furnishings depends on the space. Make well-edited choices that don't block traffic. Choose easy-care surfaces for this busy intersection. ▦

PERFECT-FOR-PARTIES
KITCHEN

REMODELED FOR COMFORT, IT'S A SPACIOUS PEOPLE PLEASER

Frequent hosts Bob and Judy Sullivan turned a tiny kitchen and little-used family room into one big entertaining—and family get-together—space.

BY SUSAN SHEETZ

The cooktop island sets up for a bountiful buffet.

The sociable Sullivans: Rob, Molly, Judy, and Bob.

FOOD PREP CORNER. *A corner appliance nook with its own outlet corrals the food processor, coffee grinder, and toaster.*

STORAGE WALL. *Parking tall cabinets on an interior wall left the spaces above the countertops for windows or art.*

The Super Bowl Party's main dish is Judy's legendary Super Bowl Chili.

PERFECT-FOR-PARTIES KITCHEN

"I like the openness the best, hands down. No matter what I'm doing, it's a social event. You never feel cut off."

—Judy Sullivan

Bob stirs up some tall tales and chili at the cooktop/buffet island.

The sitting room is a magnet for armchair quarterbacks.

Let's see, if it's January, it must be the Super Bowl Party. That's the way it goes around the Sullivan household. Despite busy careers in advertising and public relations, outgoing Bob and Judy still invite friends or business clients over at the drop of a hat—or holiday.

"I don't think a week goes by that we don't have someone over for at least dessert," says Judy. "We do formal entertaining once every five weeks, informal entertaining frequently. Having people in is our favorite thing to do."

That's not surprising, now that their circa-1900 home sports an enviably contemporary remodeled kitchen.

FAMILY GATHERING PLACE

The Sullivans' remodeling plan called for opening up the dinky kitchen to outdoor views, mill-around room for large gatherings, a minikitchen/wet bar, and generous food preparation areas.

"Most of all, we wanted the kitchen to be a special place where our family could gather and share experiences after a very busy day," says Judy.

MINIKITCHEN. Guests help themselves here to hot-and-cold snacks and drinks, leaving Judy's cooking undisturbed.

BAKING/PLANNING. The ovens stack next to the planning center because Judy doesn't use them for every meal.

PERFECT-FOR-PARTIES
KITCHEN

Rob and Molly get first licks at the postgame dessert.

The Sullivans found a pocket-size kitchen when they bought their 83-year-old home in 1985. A single window overlooked the front lawn; a family room and laundry area lurked behind the kitchen's interior partial wall. "To get from the front door to the kitchen, you had to go through an adjoining powder room or all the way around through the living room and family room," says Chicago architect Stephen Knutson.

Knutson knocked out the partial wall between the kitchen and family room for the new kitchen space. He also sealed off the kitchen's powder room door, relocated the washer and dryer, bumped out the front wall to create a sunny sitting area, and repositioned the front door.

COMFY RETREAT

Knutson geared the remodeled space for activities and tied it to the outdoors with small-pane windows and French doors. A wide archway defines the sitting room. Terra-cotta floor tile and light-bouncing white surfaces—even on the sink and faucet—create a fresh, easy mood.

"Night or day, weekday or weekend, you're never uncomfortable here," says Bob. "We can have two or three things going on: Judy cooking, me watching TV, the kids talking—but we can be together. We often say to each other, 'Isn't this a great place to be?'"

> **"The kitchen is the room that we really live in, and the rest of the house is almost incidental."**
>
> **—Bob Sullivan**

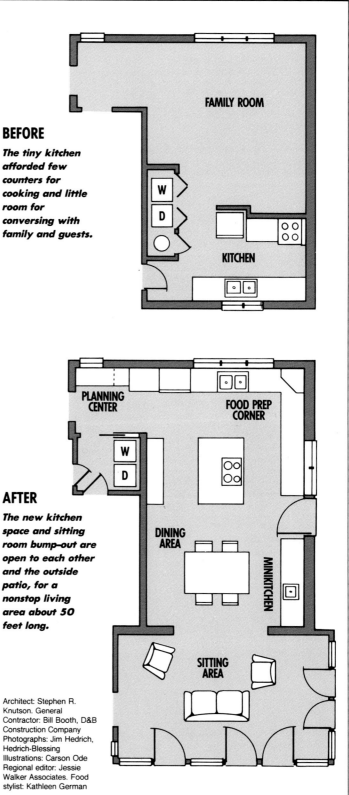

FLOOR PLANS

FAMILY ROOM

BEFORE
The tiny kitchen afforded few counters for cooking and little room for conversing with family and guests.

W / D

KITCHEN

PLANNING CENTER

FOOD PREP CORNER

W / D

AFTER
The new kitchen space and sitting room bump-out are open to each other and the outside patio, for a nonstop living area about 50 feet long.

DINING AREA

MINIKITCHEN

SITTING AREA

Architect: Stephen R. Knutson. General Contractor: Bill Booth, D&B Construction Company Photographs: Jim Hedrich, Hedrich-Blessing Illustrations: Carson Ode Regional editor: Jessie Walker Associates. Food stylist: Kathleen German

FEBRUARY

KITCHENS
WITH STYLE

BY TOM JACKSON

It's hard to describe style, but you know it when you see it. The elements of style are classic, yet the details surprise and delight you. A new twist attracts; a creative combination pleases. Here are three stylish kitchens that prove the point.

▶ Works like a kitchen, feels like a family room. Appliances and cabinets stand back, out of the traffic. The table seats eight.

▼ Plaster walls, tile wainscoting, and abundant, sun-filled windows evoke the simple, durable virtues of homes from the '20s and '30s.

▲ An arched soffit and open-end counters set the stage for a panoramic view of the backyard.

Artful Traditions

This is a kitchen for long afternoons, a magnet for family and friends. Light pours in through abundant windows and French doors. Built-out walls and a gently curved soffit ease the refrigerator and cabinets into the background. Refinished chairs and an antique table-turned-island complete the family room feeling. Come in and sit a spell. You can almost smell the fresh-baked apple pie.

Hints of history, old-fashioned charm

Crisp lines softened by warm colors

Formal in plan, this
kitchen nonetheless pro-
vides elbowroom and
gossip space for infor-
mal, impromptu parties.

PHOTOS: STEPHEN CRIDLAND. ARCHITECT: CARTER CASE ARCHITECTS. REGIONAL EDITOR: CATHY HOWARD

A Golden Glow

The layout may be square, but this spacious, honey-toned kitchen is the life of the party. A central island, replete with cooktop and sink, never fails to draw in casual conversation or volunteer cooks. The natural warmth of oak and marble balances the hard-edged lines of the cabinets and counters. Pottery and cookware behind the glass-front upper cabinets supply colorful grace notes. A bank of windows teams with an unbroken line of skylights to open the four-cornered plan into far-reaching vistas.

▼ There's room for plenty of cook's mates when you anchor guests at this island countertop.

▲ Cabinets full of Imariware and a well-stocked pot rack bring color and bustle to the design.

27

Mix black and white and ignite with

◀ A three-part skylight and triple French doors soften the hard-edged lines with a diffuse glow of natural light.

▶ High-tech track lights provide high-voltage drama near the ceiling with their stark, contemporary design.

Black Is Back

Elegant and mysterious, black conjures up images of tux-and-tails formality, after-five ambience, and uptown style. Here, all-black cabinets and appliances stand solemnly in contrast to the jazzier diamond-patterned tile and black-and-white-flecked countertops. A minimalist light fixture and knock-'em-dead red hardware complete the daring, dramatic effect. ▨

▼ Diamond tile inserts and red drawer pulls add punchy details to the monolithic scheme.

PHOTOGRAPHS: JON JENSEN. REGIONAL EDITOR: BONNIE MAHARAM

sparks of red

YOUR OWN LITTLE CORNER OF THE WORLD

BY DENISE L. CARINGER
AND SANDRA S. SORIA

Where better than the bedroom to let your own special style rise and shine? This bedtime story tells about rooms that beckon with eye-opening good looks and soul-satisfying amenities—and about furnishings you can buy to serve and soothe you. Let us help make your suite dreams come true.

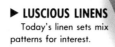

► LUSCIOUS LINENS
Today's linen sets mix
patterns for interest.

FOR A SUNNY OUTLOOK:

● Limit furnishings to a streamlined
few, such as these Shaker-like pieces.
A diligent closet replaces husky bureaus.

● Choose an airy color palette. Like
clouds against the sky, a white-against-
blue scheme is crisp but calming. Pink
brightens the cool-blue setting.

● Tailor window dressings. A simple
valance adds soft color to sleek blinds.

PHOTOGRAPHS: SCOTT LITTLE

**◄ SIMPLY
SHAKER**
Tall and slim,
this Shaker-style
chest offers stow-
ing power without
demanding floor
space.

COZY UP TO COUNTRY

After a fast-lane day, slow down with long-ago style. As warm and inviting as Granny's hugs, the bed is a passed-down family gem. Its pillow pile-up and layering of quilts add a cozy, mismatched look. Standing by, a towering armoire looks good, works hard. Sunny prints brighten dark woods.

▼ STOW IT
Its look is rooted in young America, but this piece hides modern clutter.

▶ SKIRT THE ISSUE
A well-dressed side table offers a pedestal for favorite things and a surface for writing.

◄ SWEET SHEETS
Make your bed white for fresh, crisp style. The eyelet adds old-fashioned charm.

► STRIKING LAMP
A classic candlestick lamp can lend a bright spot to any nostalgic scheme.

▼ STITCHES IN TIME
You can get the look of an antique quilt without the wait with a hand-stitched replica.

TO "AGE" YOUR ROOM:

● Set the mood with a romantic bed. Don't have an antique? Shop for an instant "heirloom" among today's reproduction bed frames.

● Top the bed with two or more prints—say, a floral and a stripe—to help your room look as if it has evolved over time.

● Forget matched furniture. Blend styles, finishes, even materials for a personal look. Add accents—a lamp, a chair, a quilt—one at a time.

SERENELY SIMPLE

Feeling burdened by too much stuff? Stash the excess to allow you, and your eyes, room to roam. In this pared-down setting, every element—snappy checks to curvy chair leg—demands attention.

▼ HEADBOARD HANG-UP

A little curve adds a lot of verve to a simple setting. Let this 40-inch-wide plaque stand in for an ornate headboard.

▶ BED CHECKS

The punch of a powerful pattern makes your bed a strong design element.

TO SIMPLIFY YOUR ROOM:

● Decide what items you really need, then pass down, sell, or store the rest.

● Make each furniture piece special. Here, family heirlooms—practical, heartwarming, and eye-catching—enliven and warm the spare setting.

● Limit pattern. Paint the walls a glowing, solid color for restfulness and to showcase each shapely furniture piece. Then splash one bold print on the bed.

◄ MIRROR IMAGE

A cheval glass reflects timeless good taste—and you!

▶ AUTHENTIC ARMCHAIR

Made famous by the first First Lady, the Martha Washington chair has thronelike presence.

PHOTOGRAPH: MIKE JENSEN. REGIONAL EDITOR: TRISH MAHARAM

SUITE ROMANCE

Like lyrics to a love song, this room soothes and delights with heart-touching sentiment. The romantic high notes include: mellow hues, a nestle-in sleep spot, an inviting chaise, and delicate lace. The ultimate warm spot? A fireplace brushed with a marble-look finish and the inspiring inscription: "Fairy tales do come true." ◼◼

◄ **STACKABLE CHESTS**
Like the right word at the right time, one special piece can spark romance in your room.

▼ **HOOKED ON RUGS**
Make old-fashioned sentiment a footnote to style with a hooked rug.

PHOTOGRAPHS: BARBARA MARTIN. REGIONAL EDITOR: MARY ANN THOMSON

TO FIND ROMANCE:

● Carve out an intimate sleeping nest. Nail together a built-in or get the feeling of one by enclosing a bed with bookshelves or a fabric canopy.

● Compose a heartwarming focal point. No fireplace? A lace-draped dressing table or a group of glowing floral prints also offer warmth.

● Add favored frills—lush fabric, wispy lace, fresh blooms—but don't overpower the senses by overcrowding a room with pattern or pieces.

SEW-SENSIBLE STYLE
A CATCHALL SEWING ROOM GETS ORGANIZED

Hemmed in by clutter that's stifling your artistic streak? Take a cue from this pretty-and-practical sewing room; it wraps up work space and stylish storage in one hardworking room.

SEW ESSENTIAL

All too often the sewing machine, like other crafts and hobby paraphernalia, is relegated to afterthought space, impossibly skimpy on storage and elbowroom. Only high-function design can mend your sewing center's inefficient ways. Take it from the creator of this airy, country-flavored work space, a veteran seamstress who delights in making everything from her family's Christmas decorations to her daughter's wedding dress. She began with the basics: an ample cutting table, storage, ironing equipment, and good lighting. Then, she packed the space with personality and perks.

NEW WORK ETHIC

Topped with a sweep of easy-care laminate, the multipurpose L-shape work center is the sewer's step- and time-saver.

● **Side-by-side sewing.** A conventional sewing machine and a serging machine (which handles long, straight seams) sit side by side on the roomy counter, always ready for a quick switch in stitching.

● **A real cutup.** Backing up to the sewing machine counter to complete the L is a 30×78-inch table for measuring fabrics and cutting patterns.

▲ Storage, work surfaces, equipment, and style are all stitched together smartly in this sewing room.

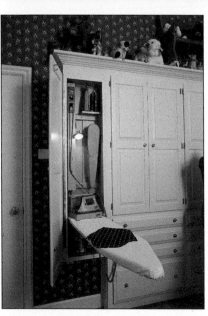

◄ Tucked into a storage wall, an ironing center speeds projects along. Drawers and doors hide clutter.

● **Stylish stower.** Beneath the table, an old document chest holds odds and ends for instant access.

● **Light for sight.** Adjustable track and countertop task lighting handle all the detail work. Then, new skylights add natural rays. The panes point east to keep this sunny space cool on summer afternoons.

TAILORED STORAGE

A wall of handsome storage conquers the inevitable sewing-room clutter. The custom-built cabinetry also offers a host of handy surprises, such as a well-stocked ironing center. A flip-down ironing board—complete with sleeve board—hides in one section, outfitted with spotlighting and a shelf for sprays and, of course, the iron. Next door, deep drawers handle yards of fabric, while layers of shallow drawers house the requisite rows of threads, bobbins, needles, and pins.

STITCHED-UP STYLE

As efficient as it is, this cozy sewing center is anything but utilitarian in style. Creamy white on the soaring ceiling, trim, cabinetry, and countertop contrasts crisply with mellow wood flooring and deep-blue, upholstered walls. It's no coincidence that the soft wall treatment (fabric stitched over quilt batting) makes an ever-ready, oversize pincushion. A menagerie of friendly stuffed animals and even the tools of the sewer's trade, such as a sheaf of yardsticks in the corner, make smile-prompting accents. ▨

MARCH

A CLEAN, SUN–

Eliminate the clutter. Simplify the lines. Unify the colors, textures, and materials.

Chris and Mary Gluck used these design concepts to transform this tiny bungalow into a cheerful, spacious-feeling home. Creating this Shakerlike simplicity can be easy and need not cost a lot of money. How? By focusing on the basics, paring away the frills, and then making the most of every detail.

BY TOM JACKSON

Chris, Erica, and Mary enjoy a sunny frolic.

White walls, natural materials, and quiet furnishings allow details—flowers and pillows—to sparkle.

New stucco dressed up the exterior.

LIGHTED PLACE

**Everything—
the apples,
chairs, dishes,
flowers, table,
and sunlight—
adds color
and plays
a role in
the design.**

A CLEAN, SUN-LIGHTED PLACE

Angled furniture and simple lines allow your eyes to roam relaxed and unencumbered. The wicker chairs can be used in either the dining or living room.

By lining up walls such as the built-in buffet and the entry bookcase, by eliminating window treatments and molding, and by recessing lighting fixtures into the ceiling, the Glucks created a house devoid of visual roadblocks or detours. A unified furnishings scheme and natural materials—wood, tile, and wicker—complete the seamless feeling. The only addition to the plan was the master bedroom.

BEFORE

AFTER

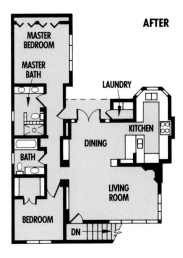

PHOTOGRAPHS: JOAN HICKS—VANDERSCHUIT. ARCHITECT: JACK SMYER ARCHITECTS, AIA. ILLUSTRATIONS: MIKE HENRY. CONTRACTOR: CHRIS GLUCK. REGIONAL EDITOR: SHARON HAVEN. SPECIAL PROPPING: SANDY GORDON, COUNTRY DOWNS

A CLEAN, SUN-LIGHTED PLACE

The kitchen cleverly manages to be both open and partially concealed. You can converse with friends in the dining area, yet hide clutter in either of two sinks. The main sink is centered in the bay window bump-out. A second sink is located behind the bar counter. Built-in appliances streamline the walls, and goods stored in the glass-front cabinets and open shelves bring color accents into the room.

Cook, converse, or clean up. The kitchen is open to views, yet quickly conceals clutter.

BEFORE

Sympathetic colors tie the house together seamlessly. White wicker chairs match the walls, and warm wood tones run from the floor to the table to the stool seats.

Two workstations at opposite ends of the kitchen give room for two cooks, despite the narrow space between the counters. Both sinks get used equally, says Chris. "We'll never go without a vegetable sink again."

A narrow kitchen is not a problem with careful planning.

A CLEAN, SUN-LIGHTED PLACE

In the master bedroom and bath, clean unbroken lines and a quiet unified look again set up a mansion-in-a-small-space feeling. Wicker and white and antique pine sound the dominant themes, with subtle touches of gray and taupe adding the grace notes. Visual volume is enhanced by several architectural elements: large windows and a vaulted ceiling in the bedroom, and a wall-to-wall mirror in the bathroom.

A wall-to-wall mirror doubles the apparent room size. The glass-block wall serves as a solid shower curtain. A recessed medicine cabinet and an unbroken expanse of granite countertop complete the uncluttered look.

Small details like door hardware and cabinet pulls repeat throughout.

Windows in the bedroom and French doors in the hall open out to courtyard views. When privacy is desired, another French door closes off the master bedroom from the hall.

One exception to the color scheme—a touch of pink for Erica.

WIDE-HORIZON KITCHEN

WRAPAROUND VIEWS OF GUESTS AND THE GARDEN

The sunny sunken bump-out coaxes guests outdoors. Up in the kitchen, an angled peninsula wraps around the center of cooking activity and displays sparkling stemware.

PHOTOGRAPHS: MIKE MORELAND. KITCHEN DESIGN: CLIFF WANG, DESIGN GALLERIA. INTERIOR DESIGN: DAYLE BARON FRIEDENBERG. REGIONAL EDITOR: RUTH L. REITER

Is your compact kitchen a fizzle at party time? Bring that wallflower to bloom with a room-size bump-out. Sink a window-walled bump-out two steps down, and you've placed your kitchen on a "pedestal." Now cooks have an overview of family and guest activities indoors and out.

Up in the kitchen, an angled, marble-top peninsula wraps around the heart of cooking activity like an elegant black-and-green ribbon, keeping kitchen helpers out of traffic flow, yet letting them participate in party patter. The counter also serves up extra storage and snacking space and acts as a pass-over to the bump-out.

Sleek white support columns and high-rise laminate cabinets amplify the mood-brightening sunlight that pours through the square-pane garden doors and windows. Remilled heart-pine floors add a cozy touch. 🏠

QUESTIONS & ANSWERS

What's on your mind? The dozens of letters we receive every month give us a pretty good idea. In fact, that's how this story begins . . .

BY DENISE L. CARINGER

QUESTION

Can we add style to our ranch's boxy living room without major remodeling?

ANSWER

Yes! Use three tactics to reshape space and add fresh character.

▶ **TURN THE TABLES** and seating pieces into a room-widening diagonal. Float this on-the-bias grouping away from the walls, and you'll have the makings of a fresh, surprisingly spacious look.

▶ **HIT THE CEILING** with lofty focal-point shelves.

▶ **GET MELLOW.** Serene neutrals, from paint to fabrics, set a mood that's relaxing and expansive.

An angled, "off-the-wall" furniture arrangement helps open up a once-boxy, ranch-house living room.

PHOTOGRAPHS: GENE JOHNSON. DESIGN: JAN THORNTON. REGIONAL EDITOR: NANCY E. INGRAM

QUESTION

"We've just bought our first home, and we have almost no furniture. How can we get a great look now without buying cheap things that we'll have to replace later?"

ANSWER

First, don't panic! Just start with some flexible basics that will not only grow and change as you do, but will look absolutely wonderful right now.

▶ **HAVE A SEAT.** Instead of blowing the budget on one new sofa, furnish an entire sitting spot with four wicker chairs. Their airiness is just right for small spaces, and their classic look makes them adaptable building blocks for future decorating.

▶ **SHOW YOUR STRIPES.** Besides setting the mood and lending up-to-the-minute style, these hot fabrics rivet the eye and, thus, help "fill" empty spaces.

▶ **CUT A RUG.** A homemade canvas floor-cloth puts pattern at your feet—without bringing your budget to its knees. Yes, you *can* do it yourself!

▶ **FIRE UP.** Painted and simply leaned against the wall, an old fireplace surround warms any room with architectural romance—instantly. Look for similar ones at antiques shops and flea markets.

▶ **TAKE A BREATHER.** Open space is essential to any successful scheme, so don't worry about filling every bit of the room.

◀ **BREAK THE RULES.** Instead of the expected dining pieces, an outdoor table and grid chairs make perfect, summer-house companions to the living room furnishings. Bonus: they're easy to find, small in scale, low in cost.

◀ **HANG IN THERE.** Bright posters play up the color scheme with images that enhance that peaceful, easy feeling. Busy? You can order the posters—framed!—from a mail-order catalog.

Summery furnishings open up a tiny dining room.

PHOTOGRAPHS: PERRY STRUSE. DESIGN: DENISE L. CARINGER

QUESTION

"I like decorating with the things we collect, but our place is looking more like a flea market than a home. How can we pull things together?"

ANSWER

Start by paring your collectibles so that one mood prevails, then group related items for maximum decorative impact.

Antiques charm a basic bungalow.

▶ **GO ON A DESIGN DIET.** Don't try to live with everything you own or love—especially if you *love* everything! Instead, decide on a mood, summon your willpower, and weed out things that no longer fit. Here, the unassuming beauty of handcrafted pieces is the tie that binds.

▶ **PUT ANTIQUES TO WORK.** When space is tight, you can't afford to merely display antique furnishings. More than pretty faces, these dining room chairs, walnut table, and storage pieces earn their keep—every day.

▶ **KEEP THE BACKGROUND SIMPLE.** Plain painted walls, instead of busily patterned ones, showcase each prized collectible.

▶ **GET ORGANIZED.** Group companion pieces, instead of spreading them around. Just inside the front door, an extended family of treasured quilts abides happily within a painted quilt cupboard. The result? Cohesiveness—not clutter.

A stunning lineup of quilts welcomes all who enter.

PHOTOGRAPHS: BARBARA MARTIN. FIELD EDITOR: MARY ANNE THOMSON

COZY STYLE
An aged work-table plays host to antique chairs. Above the pie safe, pewter plates and earthy jugs make a strong but succinct statement.

QUESTION

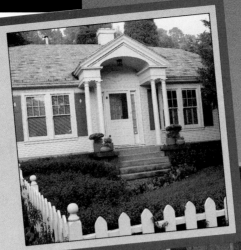

"We bought an old bungalow for its cozy character, not its size. How can we make the small living room comfortable and homey without its appearing overstuffed?"

ANSWER

Relax with these tried-and-true decorating tactics:

▶**LIGHTEN UP.** Keep things airy with white walls, a slim pedestal end table, and wicker chairs that you can see through—and *under*.

▶**REACH FOR THE CEILING.** Point the way up, and you'll be less likely to see the limited floor space below. An armoire corrals clutter and, like the torchère's beam, raises your sights.

▶**BE A SHUTTER BUG.** Unlike heavy draperies or curtains, natural shutters provide privacy and cottage charm without intruding on space.

▼**GO WITH THE FLOW** of space and light. This open-arm chair and leggy table offer vintage style without walling things up. 🏠

Airy furniture maintains a spacious look.

PHOTOGRAPHS: LAURIE BLACK, ROSLYN BANISH/ARX. FIELD EDITOR: BARBARA CATHCART

**EASYGOING
ATMOSPHERE**
Open wall and
floor spaces give
your spirit room to
roam and your
body space to
breathe. Even your
eyes get a break.

A PLACE FOR EVERYTHING

STORAGE IDEAS FOR ALL AROUND YOUR KITCHEN

BY SUSAN SHEETZ

▲ AND EVERYTHING IN ITS PLACE

Poor kitchen storage can take the joy out of cooking. So can dated cabinet and countertop materials and tired appliances. Avid cooks Judy and Frank Weigel shook their ranch kitchen out of its stagnant 1950s mind-set with a 1990s-oriented remodeling. The Weigels' sleek white kitchen restyling and cleverly devised storage organizers are good lessons to follow as you plan your own more-efficient kitchen.

◀ STAPLE-STASHING BAKE CENTER

How organized can a baking center be? At countertop level, twin tambour-door niches corral any idle appliances. Then base cabinet storage lines up with four-star efficiency. First in line, a large cutting board slides out for a variety of baking activities. Then comes the cutlery drawer, followed by a divided drawer that holds baking equipment and pans. On the bottom, compartments of acrylic plastic sheets sort flour, sugar, pasta, and legumes.

◀ TOO-HOT-TO-HANDLE LANDING PAD

Because her microwave and conventional ovens are stacked, Judy asked for a pullout wooden board between them. "It's so handy to simply set a dish or pan down when baking," she says. When she's done with the landing pad, she slides it away like a breadboard.

▲ SMALL-SPACE STORAGE PLACE

Even a smidgen of wall space can be put to good use. "I love this small counter area," says Judy. "It's great for every day when we load and unload the refrigerator." This mighty-mite storage spot includes another deep drawer divided with acrylic plastic sheets for organizing such easy-to-lose items as cookware lids and muffin pans.

◀ RACK UP SOME CORNER STORAGE

Check out adjacent spaces close to the kitchen for storage. This wine-and-crystal cabinet built-in tucks into a niche between the back door and the kitchen proper. Wine bottles rest, properly tilted downward, in special slots beneath the shelves. There's even a display nook for the wine "de-corker."

Design/Contractor: Martha Kerr, C.K.D., Neil Kelly Co. Photographs: Steve Cridland Regional editor: Cathy Howard

ROOM TO MANEUVER
REMOVING THE BARRIERS TO EASY LIVING

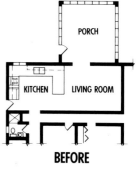

PORCH

KITCHEN   LIVING ROOM

BEFORE

DECK   LIVING ROOM

KIT.   DINING ROOM

AFTER

▲ "All ages can use our home," says Mary Helen Hayes. "The openness really suits our lives now."

▶ A raised hearth gives Gerry easy access to the no-hassle gas fireplace.

▼ Gerry's wheelchair slips easily into the stepped peninsula's 8-inch toe space.

Persons new to wheelchairs often find immediate obstacles to easy living indoors. Just ask Gerry Hayes. About late in life with a spinal virus left Gerry with the need for a wheelchair. Suddenly he and wife Mary Helen found their three-story home impractical.

TURN TO ONE STORY

The Hayeses solved the problem by remodeling their cramped, one-story summer cabin into a year-round, accessible, and barrier-free home. Minneapolis designers Mary McCary and Connie Nelson came up with a plan that enlarged passageways, removed some walls and angled others, and transformed a three-season porch into a living room with four additional feet and comfy amenities.

In the kitchen, a custom his-and-her peninsula makes everyday and special mealtime preparations more efficient. This bi-level, easy-to-clean laminate counter houses a second sink, drawers for Gerry's kitchen gear, and an under-the-counter refrigerator. It's also a buffet for nearby dining and a quick-snack bar for grandkids.

An expandable, apronless dining table allows Gerry's wheelchair to move in close. Tough, attractive commercial-grade vinyl wall covering repels scuffs from chair wheels. The maple floors blend with low-looped commercial carpet for free wheeling throughout the house. ▦

Interior design: Mary McCary, ASID, and Connie Nelson, In-House Design
Contractor: Metro Build Tech. Regional editor: Bernadette Baczynski

APRIL

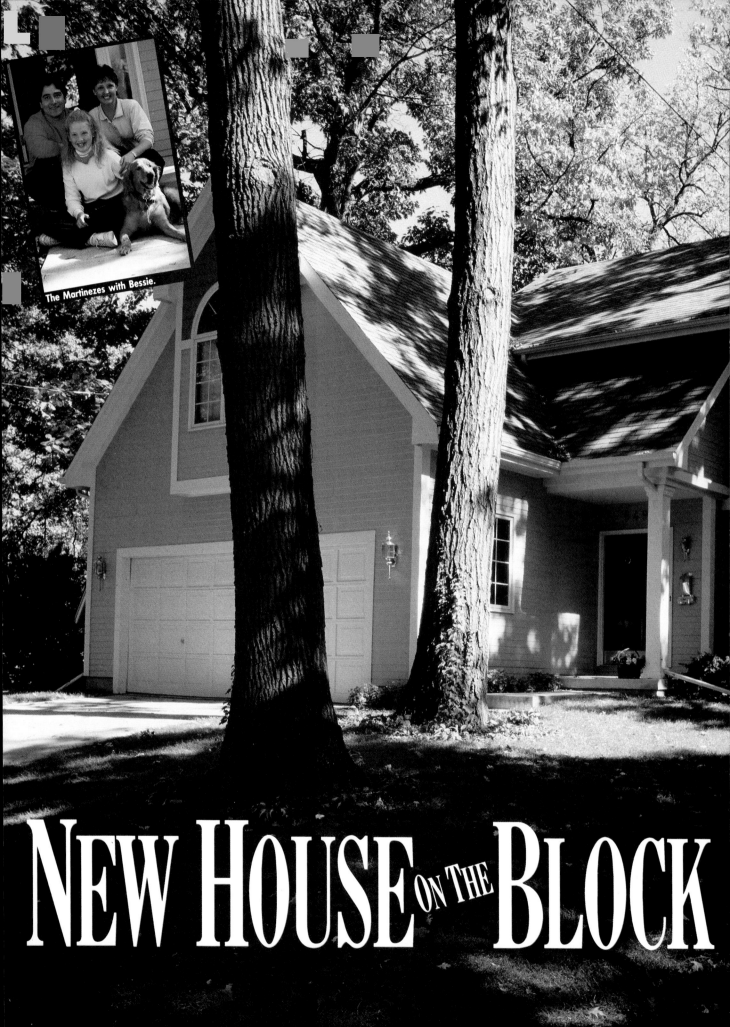

The Martinezes with Bessie.

NEW HOUSE ON THE BLOCK

The Martinezes' new house borrows period trappings from older homes in its 1920s-era Des Moines neighborhood: deep eaves, a steep roof, gabled dormers.

G
randma's four-poster will look right at home. So will your VCR. Old and new can merge comfortably when you build your dream home on a vintage street.

BY WILLIAM L. NOLAN
AND TOM JACKSON

Lattice fencing and a one-story wing yield luxurious privacy for the deck out back.

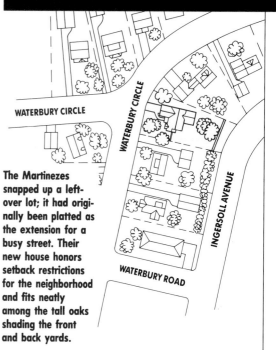

WATERBURY CIRCLE

WATERBURY CIRCLE

INGERSOLL AVENUE

WATERBURY ROAD

The Martinezes snapped up a left-over lot; it had originally been platted as the extension for a busy street. Their new house honors setback restrictions for the neighborhood and fits neatly among the tall oaks shading the front and back yards.

YESTERYEAR'S SETTING, TODAY'S PERKS

A little luck helped Des Moines remodelers Ann and Rick Martinez snag the perfect site for their new home: a leftover lot originally pegged for extension of a thoroughfare. Sensitive planning mated the new house with its setting. Ann studied the rooflines, detailing, and exterior colors of nearby homes, and shaped the plan to honor setbacks and preserve the site's glorious old oaks.

> "I do a lot of design work at home, and the windows and French doors in the dining room lend great natural light."
>
> —ANN PATTERSON MARTINEZ

Building from scratch meant the Martinezes could add amenities that older homes usually lack, such as an efficient kitchen layout and open-plan living areas. Minimal partitions let the main-floor rooms flow together around a central hall. The only visual boundary is a built-in buffet flanked by oblong columns. Jogs in the exterior wall help define living, dining, and family spaces, and a super-size island buffers the kitchen from the central traffic corridor. High ceilings give the roominess an added boost; big windows let the light spill in.

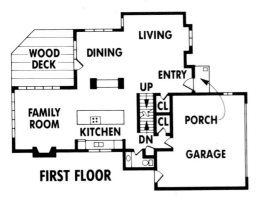

FIRST FLOOR

WOOD DECK · DINING · LIVING · ENTRY · UP · CL · CL · PORCH · FAMILY ROOM · KITCHEN · DN · GARAGE

▲ Ann's plan banishes the boxed-in feeling typical of older homes. The main spaces flow around a pair of columns carrying the second floor.

French doors put ▶ the dining room, family room, and kitchen just a step away from the deck and garden.

Busy schedules take a back seat to sunny comfort in the family room. The TV fits flush in one end of the kitchen island; work space on top offers a landing pad for snacks.

Wintry evenings find
the Martinezes
toasting their toes
near the fire. Check-
erboard tile tempers
the mantel's fluted
elegance; built-ins
house books, games,
a flip-down desk.

Early-1900s floor plans isolated the kitchen from family living spaces, an arrangement that's totally out of step with the 1990s. To make the most of precious hours when the family relaxes at home, the Martinezes merged their kitchen and family room, putting hearthside sitting space just a few feet from the work area. This makes it easy for the family to catch up with each other at day's end, even while getting dinner ready.

SOUL-SOOTHING WARMTH

A vintage-style mantel helps the fireplace deliver welcome-home warmth and a nostalgic focal point for the family room. The mantel's proportions and detailing echo turn-of-the-century forerunners; a melon-pink wall and a checkerboard band of ceramic tile add contemporary punch.

ON-TAP KITCHEN CONVENIENCE

Ann chose a galley-style layout for arm's-reach convenience in the kitchen, but added a few extra inches between the cleanup and island work centers so that two cooks could work comfortably without colliding.

A super-size island diverts traffic around the work area. The island has become "action central" for the household: a food prep area, a bake center, an informal eating area, and an impromptu perch for family and guests. It's topped with four different surfaces to handle the various functions: stainless steel on the cooktop; ceramic tile for parking hot pans; butcherblock for cutting, rolling, and slicing; and laminate for dining and serving.

"The island was built with two or more cooks in mind, and for our laid-back style of entertaining. We call it our bowling alley."

—ANN AND RICK MARTINEZ

▲ Ann outfitted the island for easy-does-it cooking and baking: microwave and conventional ovens, a glide-out trash bin, and a multiple-outlet strip for small appliances.

◄ The cooktop, sink, and refrigerator are just a step or two apart, but work space abounds on the island— enough for a bevy of cook's helpers!

> " **O**ur clients often complain that they need a bigger bathroom, so we decided to treat ourselves to a large, full-service bath."
> —**RICK MARTINEZ**

SECOND FLOOR

MASTER BATH · MASTER BEDROOM · WALK-IN CLOSET · UP · BEDROOM · DN · BEDROOM · LAUN

▲ Two large bedrooms, a family bath, and the master suite share the central hall upstairs. Storage and circulation space helps deaden noise between rooms.

Katie's room has ▶ floor space to spare for daytime play. Her window ledge is home base for favorite toys and games.

Photographs: Perry Struse Architect: Ann Patterson Martinez. Regional editor: Mary Didio. Illustrations: Mike Henry

PRECIOUS PRIVACY

Grand old homes of the early 1900s had two virtues in short supply today: roominess and privacy. The Martinezes resurrected these benefits in their new home by giving all the rooms generous proportions and by buffering the bedrooms against noise. Vaulted ceilings lend extra stretch in the master suite and Katie's bedroom. Arched windows in each room soar into the gabled exterior wall, framing views of the oaks outside.

The bedrooms cluster pinwheel-fashion around the central hall, each tucked into a separate wing beneath the multigabled roof. Bathrooms and closets work with the central hall to deaden noise between rooms.

ONE-STOP MASTER BATH

Grandma's bath may have been just as big, but today's version is much more lavishly appointed. Rick and Ann outfitted theirs with a whirlpool tub, a separate shower compartment, a double-bowl vanity, and a mirrored closet. There's room at one end for an exercise bike, and the storage wall includes a niche for the TV. ▪

WHITE-HOT DESIGN
SURPRISING ELEMENTS BRIGHTEN A SUN-ROOM

A bit of surprise can mean the difference between a good room and a grand one. In this sun-room, unexpected furnishings and frills please the senses—but still fulfill a practical mission.

DEFINE YOUR SPACE

Sun-rooms harbor split personalities—they're part front porch, part living room. That's great, but how do you decide whether your decor should appeal to the indoor side of the room's personality or to its kinship with the great outdoors?

A fat-and-sassy sofa and elementary geometry give an architecturally grand sun-room a sense of humor.

Before you choose the latter—a path that usually leads to wicker, matchstick blinds, and potted palms—why not consider a road less traveled? This sun-room shows there's more than one way to tap tradition.

VIVE LA DIFFÉRENCE

Delightfully different and easily adaptable elements can refresh any sun-room:

● **Have fun.** With nary a stick of patio furniture, this sun-room still offers outdoor spirit. Lively geometrics bring the lightheartedness of a playground to the space. Color and whimsy are sure-fire room sparkers.

● **Comfort comes first.** Furnished with living-room-caliber pieces, the space offers indoor comforts. Still,

Made to match the bench's cutouts, pillows repeat a geometric refrain.

the camelback sofa and easy chair look casual dressed in fun-loving wraps. The point here? Don't limit yourself to a certain furniture style just because of a room's location.

● **Smile-evoking accents.** Unexpected accessories give the space one-of-a-kind character. A planter as an end table, a homemade wooden necklace as a drapery tieback, and geometric pillows tossed around are bright ideas, easily duplicated.

● **Clean backgrounds.** A white backdrop provides a crisp canvas for the jolts of color sprinkled throughout the room. Left bare, windows show off artful architecture and let the sun shine in. White paint and undressed windows help any sun-room see the light. ▦

"Decorating is more fun when you have limited funds ... you have to be creative." —JONI

BEAUTY
AND THE
BUDGET

DECORATING WITH MORE LOVE THAN MONEY

Have a decorating budget that just won't budge? So did the Ruff family. Joni and Jim's solution? Substitute creativity for cash. Come on in and help yourself to their mind-over-money ideas.

BY SANDRA S. SORIA

The Ruffs: Jim, Joni, young Jason, and Patches.

BEAUTY
AND THE
BUDGET

"Older homes have more character built right in." —JONI

Packed with personality and easy-do ideas, the Ruffs' Oregon home is a textbook on affordable style. Its lessons are A-B-C simple: start with clean backdrops; stock with pieces with a personal past; sprinkle with lively accessories. Here, creamy walls and gleaming planks showcase inherited sofas, home-sewn pillows, and a few eye-grabbing accents for a warm, heartfelt look.

Perched atop a whitewashed mantel, a trio of birdhouses tickles the eye. Nearby, mismatched candlesticks also huddle together for more impact.

Passed-down family pieces form the heart of the Ruff home. Joni had her grandparents' sofas cloaked in fresh fabrics of her choosing.

RUFF IDEAS

■ Coat walls in creamy white paint to make small spaces live larger than life. White also bounces light around the room to play up sunshine.

■ Revive antiques with new fabrics or finishes to gain quality furnishings at a bargain price.

■ Search out a local carpenter to help you create one-of-a-kind style on a budget. Joni had the birdhouses built for a song; she finished them with paint.

Complete Poems

E. E. CUMMINGS   Harcourt

CLASS REUNION

"I love white; it's clean, bright, pretty." —JONI

RUFF IDEAS

■ Splurge on backdrops; simplify furniture. The Ruffs spent money on French doors, flooring, and wallpaper; saved with wicker and family hand-downs.

■ Look for accents anywhere. Splashed with paint and draped in lace, a floor mat is promoted to a wall hanging.

■ Do it yourself. Jim stripped cupboards, removed doors, and revived them with white for a refreshing, low-cost look.

BEAUTY AND THE BUDGET

Adding service with style, an antique flour bin creates a welcome, woodsy island in a sea of cool white.

New chicken wire, shirred fabric panels, and fresh paint bring an old pie safe up to date.

Sheet vinyl puts classic style underfoot—and the Ruffs under budget. Outlined in black and white, home-sewn cushions add snap to the space.

"My mother taught me about clutter. Her lesson is simple: If you don't use it, get rid of it." —JONI

RUFF IDEAS

■ Coat with white for an instant update. White enamel works modern wonders on a dated and dull waterbed frame.

■ Use barely-there window covers for utterly simple style. Here, a roller blind disappears by day and provides privacy by night.

■ Compose one-of-a-kind collages from adored objects. A summer hat, treasured chest, and arty poster speak softly of lives and loves.

BEAUTY AND THE BUDGET

A narrow ledge offers an artful poster a place to stand, plus adds architectural oomph to the boxy room.

As serene as still water, this all-white waterbed practically insists that you dive in. Precious and few accents give the room an endearing personality without spoiling its simple pleasure.

This chest-on-chest began life as two unfinished bureaus. Joni removed the smaller one's legs, bathed the two in white, then stacked them for stowing power with style.

If simplicity is the motto for the Ruffs' school of budget-conscious design, then white paint is the mascot. The couple lavishes the liquid on walls and furnishings, loving how it visually uncramps small quarters and freshens what it touches. Against the gallery-white backdrop, furnishings stand out like works of art. To preserve the lean, clean look, they limit the home's residents to a chosen few, including pampered plants and something-special accents. "Accessories mean a lot," says Joni. "You can add personality by using things that say something about you *and* to you—books, pictures, family treasures."

BEAUTY
AND THE
BUDGET

RUFF IDEAS

■ **Soften with greenery; color with blooms.** "Plants naturally warm a room," says Joni.

■ **Add a personal touch with easy-sew curtains, pillows, and duvet cover** (made from two panels of 96-inch-wide decorator fabrics).

■ **Create vintage architecture with a stock-molding chair rail and a romantic wall covering.**

Visitors get treated to the home's soft and soothing spirit in an under-the-eaves guest room. Here, the humble and the handmade mingle with grace. The iron headboard once served on Joni's grandparents' Oregon farm. Joni stitched bedcovers in striking stripes to hug her guests with sunny warmth. ◫

Old-fashioned gestures "romance" this guest room: wispy eyelet, a simple but serviceable pegboard, and sun-dipped colors.

MAY

BY
DENISE L. CARINGER,
ROBERT E. DITTMER,
AND
SANDRA S. SORIA

BETTER HOMES AND GARDENS®
AND BUTTERICK PRESENT

ROOM FRESHENERS

It's *sew* easy to perk up your winter-weary spaces. With these *Butterick* patterns and your fabric, you'll have your rooms in stitches. These sew-your-own projects are as quick as spring lightning to make and just as flashy. Look how sassy stripes and plump pillows—plus coats of white paint—coaxed this porch out of its dreary mood in a hurry.

BEFORE

"BEFORE" PHOTOGRAPHS: PERRY STRUSE. "AFTER" PHOTOGRAPHS: SCOTT LITTLE

AFTER.
Stitch curtain rings to the top and bottom of fabric panels to create a fresh and unflappable shield from the sun—or from a dismal view. Slide the rings onto sturdy dowels, and secure them with screw-in hooks.

LIGHTENED-UP LIVING ROOM

Given a one-two punch of color and pattern, this slug-gish living room really snapped to. Dressed in blushing but bold striped linen, plain panes become dynamic dec-orative players. The simple-sew side curtains tumble gracefully from artful, oversize *Kirsch* rods and rings to soften the setting and give it a needed vertical lift. Decked in checks and stripes, a playful jumble of pillows relaxes *Bernhardt*'s classic sofa. The pillow covers slip on like pinafores; tailor them to old cushions to change your furniture's mood on a whim. Even the ottoman gets friendlier when a cheery, scalloped shawl is tossed on.

BEFORE

Pattern package:
No. 4895

80

DRESSED-UP DINING ROOM

BEFORE

Who says a formal dining room can't have fun? Choose friendly fabrics, then use these patterns to dress bare chairs and stark surfaces in outfits as crisp and casual as a cotton sundress. You'll make every meal a picnic.

AFTER.
Spring rains can't dampen this room's sunny mood, thanks to sew-your-own covers in happy, cotton-candy colors.

Pattern package:
No. 4895

Make this pleated shade to brighten a plain lamp.

BY
SANDRA S.
SORIA

SAY "SO LONG"
TO THE BLAND
DINETTE SET.
Now we're
cooking with
friendlier
furnishings and
spicier accents.
These kitchen
eating spots
offer fresh
recipes for
stay-awhile
style.

ROUND THE KITCHEN TABLE

ROOM PHOTOGRAPH: KIM BRUN. ARCHITECT: BOKAL, KELLEY-MARKHAM. REGIONAL EDITOR: SHARON HAVEN. CHAIR PHOTOGRAPH: BOB DALTON

83

ROUND THE KITCHEN TABLE

Fond memories of Swedish farmhouse tables laden with hearty fare prompted this simply charming eating spot. A clean white backdrop, mellow pine, friendly wicker, and moody-blue fabrics create the look.

To perk up a room with personality, put yourself in the picture. Surround the people you know and the places you've been with colorful, textural borders, such as these mail-order, cut-to-fit frames.
Buying information, page 00.

Kitchens warmed by sentiment naturally become the heart of the home. Here, a gallery of family photos lovingly looks over the shoulder of an old-favorite antique bench.
Photographs: Mike Jensen
Regional editor: Trish Maharam

Spice an eating spot with unexpected seating. More than just a pretty piece, this bench lends comfort and function—the seat lifts to reveal a storage well.
Photograph: Bob Dalton

Put traditional pieces in a nontraditional place for a new twist on an old look. Steps from the stove, this elegant grouping relaxes when flanked by friendly fabrics, lightened-up walls, and undressed panes that invite the garden inside. The result? A spot grand enough for a multicourse meal and cozy enough for burgers with the kids.

Reproductions bring the most exquisite 18th-century styles within reach. These chairs off the old block offer the verve of flowing, classic curves.

Photograph: Bill Ellis

Resist the urge to put fair-weather furniture by a greenhouse wall. Instead, a formal setup offers curious contrast. Another surprise, slip-covered director's chairs put armchair comfort in a tight spot.

Photograph: Maxwell MacKenzie. Regional editor: Eileen A. Deymier

Want a change of pace in a traditional dining place? Use the room for lounging as well as dining. Then, add an area rug—like this light and lively dhurrie—to set the two areas apart.

Start with a crisp backdrop, toss in texture, sprinkle with collectibles, and you have the makings of a savory eating spot. As any good cook knows, though, the secret to a successful mix is careful measuring. For a palatable palette, lavish on basic white, then pepper with zesty black and a dash of color.

Bring the charm of a sidewalk café to your kitchen by inviting outdoor shapes inside for supper. Cast in an indoor role, this iron chair offers a delicate, natural flavor with its fine-lined shape and weathered, verdigris patina.
Photograph: Bob Dalton

Just as nuts add spunk to a bowl of ice cream, a contrast of textures adds visual spirit to a room. Here, woven rush seats and a grainy marble-top table stand out in a crowd of slick laminate cabinetry and vinyl flooring.
Photograph: Vanderschuit Studio. Regional editor: Sharon Haven

Parade favorite things to excite a space with color and personality. Even everyday objects, such as new Fiesta ware, become works of art when put proudly on display.

To cozy up a too-sterile kitchen, let it bask in the glow of warm colors, such as yellow or red. Then add golden waves of wood grains and friendly wicker to give an eating place all the warmth of summer sunshine.
Photograph: Timothy Fields. Design: Carol Siegmeister. Regional editor: Eileen A. Deymier

Mix new painted pieces with wood goods for visual vitality. This pie safe wears fashionable yellow to lend service with style.
Photograph: Bill Ellis

B reak free from the matched-set mind-set. Because they share chunky shapes and a casual outlook, these amicable pieces get along fine without looking alike. ▦

JUNE

MIXING BUSINESS WITH LEISURE

HOW TO FURNISH ONE ROOM FOR BOTH

When Barbara Steele of Minneapolis moved her family into a four-room cottage, the challenge was to create a comfortable home *and* find space in it for a home office. Here's how she accomplished the task, proving that you can live comfortably in limited space while you nurture a child and a business. Take a few notes on decorating from the main room of Barbara's cottage:

● **Organize function first.** Remember the central space of yesteryear's log cabin where child care, dining, business, and conversation took place? As hearths were long ago, this hearth is the hub around which all other furnishings revolve. It provides a focal point for a conversation island, allowing a natural traffic flow from the sliding doors through the room. The sideline seating arrangement frees up the opposite wall for a desk and dining setup. A little one can run freely around furnishings, hide behind love seats, and plop down for naps.

If you have no focal point such as a fireplace to anchor a seating island, create one with a tall armoire or modular unit that houses media equipment or shelf units that hold a library of books.

● **Plan for big comfort.** Wrap the room in pale pine boards to set a casual mood. The natural color and smooth texture of the wood panels keep the walls from "moving in."

When space is tight, think small about furnishings. Instead of the standard 8-foot sofa, choose two hospitable love seats that offer more room-arranging flexibility and sink-in sitting. Or, use four big armchairs or compact modulars to define a conversation area. Bind the seating together with a foot-warming area rug.

● **Choose double-duty pieces** to furnish work and play activities. This durable, tile-top table serves up dinner or a game for four when it's pulled into the traffic path. Pushed against the wall for most of the day, it works hard to organize business affairs and to tackle telephone tasks. ▦

Wide-awake wood sheds light on this double-life desk and table.

Double your work-and-play pleasures with a backdrop of natural elements. Then, think twice about the functions of the space and the furnishings you'll need to provide for comfort and work.

PHOTOGRAPHS: SUSAN GILMORE. DESIGN: BARBARA STEELE. REGIONAL EDITOR: BERNADETTE BACZYNSKI

SHIPSHAPE SPACE

How to stow away in style

A computer desk at the end of the shelf unit reports for homework duty. A stool slides under the desktop.

This 7 × 8½-foot room shows that you can transform a "shoe-box" space into efficient and comfortable quarters without sacrificing style.

Bet your child won't hang clothes on the floor or lose a CD in the clutter after you organize with built-ins. To improve a small space, treat it to light-and-airy colors, a creative use of space, and hardworking, custom-made furnishings.

Here are five strategies for shaping up a small space without shipping out high-style decorating in the process:

A trimmed-up platform bed tucks in under a window covered with the slimmest of mini-blinds. Up top, the room's occupant has private sleeping quarters by night and a cheery sofa by day. Down below, ample drawers under the bed stash pajamas, pillows, and blankets during the day.

Open shelving to the ceiling emphasizes the height of the room while playing down its narrow width. Hung over the built-in drawer units, it fills the wall beside the bed with vertical storage. The shelving commandeers books, pictures, and personal belongings. With its eye turned toward the bed and comfortable viewing, the television fits compactly into the lower section of the shelf unit.

Wide drawers under the shelving unit along the bedroom wall replace a bulky dresser for clothing and other personal belongings. The lines of the built-ins keep the room uncluttered and easy to clean.

A floating shelf desk covered with plastic laminate slips in as a computer and printer space and the upholstered stool slides away under the shelf when it's not in use. When handwritten homework needs to be done, the lightweight computer and printer can be moved to the side.

Hard-wearing industrial carpet laid wall to wall puts the final touch on the orderly space. The color adds the bonus of not showing dirt. ▨

JULY

LET THE
SUNSHINE in

HOW A SMALL SPACE SEES THE LIGHT

Like most rooms these days, this Tulsa hot spot is asked to do a whole lot of living. It cooks, serves meals, entertains guests, and even relaxes you after a long day. Just how does a small space do it all? This busy one-room guesthouse succeeds by packing in the service, then playing up the fun. Want to cajole any hardworking room into a lighthearted mood? Let these bright ideas show you the way.

BY

SANDRA S.

SORIA

PHOTOGRAPHS: GENE JOHNSON. ARCHITECT: JACK ARNOLD, AIA. INTERIOR DESIGN: SUSAN ANDERSON SWANSON. REGIONAL EDITOR: NANCY E. INGRAM

In a multiuse room, furnishings act like walls to divide and

cozy up space. Facing off to the fireplace, the sofa and chest

duo draws the line between living and dining spots, then area

rugs define and anchor the groupings.

LET THE SUNSHINE IN

To put wiry electronics out of sight when they're out of mind, BUILT-IN CABINETS stand at the ready. For a buy-now option, look for modular shelving units or armoires. Tuck the clutter-cutters into your room's niches, or use them as visual anchors to arrange furniture groupings.

Aged to a vintage texture, NATURAL adds old-shoe comfort and familiarity to a room. Side tables stand on RUGGED IRON legs, another touchable element that relaxes the room's attitude.

Brighten a room's outlook by inviting the sun in regularly. Tucked under the eaves, **TRANSOM WINDOWS** raise the roof for a peek at the swaying treetops and blue sky. The well-placed touch of glass also lets the room look larger than life. For more natural light, the owners went to great panes: **WALLS OF GLASS** flood the space with sunshine; then, **PLANTATION SHUTTERS** with pop-out transoms direct the mighty rays and add Casablanca charm.

To keep things light, avoid weighing down a scheme with heavy furniture. A sturdy **WICKER SOFA** and see-through **SLATTED CHAIRS** leaven this grouping, but don't sacrifice cushiony comfort. In a surprise move, the sofa even pulls out into a queen-size bed to rest guests.

I REMEMBER AMERICA

LET THE SUNSHINE IN

Taking cues from the sand and the sea, this interior lives like a breezy getaway spot. Sandy, TAUPE PAINT coaxes walls to stretch out like an expanse of beach. Natural beauties, earthy TERRA-COTTA flooring and CERAMIC tiles, offer smooth surfaces to reflect light, adding to the wide-open feeling. The LIGHTWEIGHT RATTAN dining set takes the mind to a seaside resort, and doesn't gobble up much space. Even accessories, such as the tropical houseplant and seaside painting, support the space's fun-in-the-sun attitude.

The room's **EXPOSED ARCHITECTURE** adds eye appeal and volume to the pint-size area. Perched on trusses, **SPOTLIGHTS** point out the soaring ceiling. Then, a trio of **HANGING LIGHTS** defines the kitchen work area, setting it aglow. **GLASS-FRONT CABINETS** also boost the sense of spaciousness.

For gutsy good looks, lay style on the line. **BOLD STRIPES** power the scheme with playful cabaña spirit. Because too much of one pattern can be dizzying, a kindred **FLAME STITCH** fabric steps over the lines and blazes with more colors. Stain-proof cotton fabrics lend easy-care comfort.

NEW SPACE DISCOVERIES
SPECIAL USES FOR NOOKS AND CRANNIES

Cozy up with a book in a cushioned cranny. Inside, add a reading light and bookshelf. Oh, and don't forget the cordless phone.

Feather a skylghted nest under the eaves. Include shelves for organized stashing.

Seek out the hidden spaces at your house and turn them into private getaways or recesses that work hard to keep you organized. Take a look under the eaves, on a landing, or between a pair of walls.

Any two walls, even the end walls of a pair of bookcases, create a nook or cranny. Place a seat beneath a window with a bookcase on each side and you'll have a nook for dreaming, catnaps, and street-watching. For snuggling up Scandinavian style, build a daybed between two bumped-out walls (*above*).

View angled spaces in a new light. Could they become a shelter from the storm, a reading-and-writing retreat, a homework station for a student? Consider decorating under basement stairs and attic dormers. The office (*left*) tucks neatly away on a landing at the top of the stairs.

Easy

DECORATING

Breezy

WITH

Summer

SHEETS

Style

BY DENISE L. CARINGER

ROBERT E. DITTMER AND SANDRA S. SORIA

AH-H-H...SUMMERTIME AND THE LIVING IS EASY. WANT TO HANG ONTO THAT FEELING YEAR-ROUND?

TURN THE PAGE FOR SIMPLE-TO-SEW DECORATING IDEAS THAT BREATHE OCEAN-BREEZE FRESHNESS INTO LANDLOCKED ROOMS. ALL SEWN WITH LINENS DESIGNED BY LIBERTY OF LONDON FOR *MARTEX (SHOWN ABOVE)*, THESE IDEAS ARE EASY ON THE BUDGET, TOO.

Easy Breezy Summer Style

A BEDROOM CAN enjoy sheet success almost overnight with these wonderfully fresh fabric treatments as agents of change. Love a happy ending? Look how the table skirt, cushion covers, and floor-screen curtain (*below*)—sewn from linens—"romance" a once-lonely corner.

WITH LINES THAT DIP AND CURVE like a gently rolling sea, sheet-draped walls calm a room. Then, prints and textures as varied as pebbles on the beach perk it up with personality.

FOR A TUCKED-IN FEELING as good as Mom used to give, look for linens that

Easy Breezy Summer Style

SEW-EASY COVER-UPS and mixable linens make a dynamic decorating duo. They'll save a room by reviving tired furniture or making matches of unlikely pieces.

pamper with little extras.
Liberty of London designs
for *Martex* invite with lacy
trims, delicate prints, and
a medley of ready-made
throw pillows.

INSIDE OR OUT, curvy wicker plumped with blooming, sew-your-own cushions says summer fresh. Another tip for giving your rooms charming cottage appeal? Start with clean, white backdrops.

Easy Breezy Summer Style

TIE BACK the wall coverings at the window for a peek at the great outdoors.

CRISP STRIPED sheets hang by ribbons from porcelain pulls. The covering can be easily lifted off for washing.

Photographs: D. Randolph Foulds. Location: The Summer House, Nantucket, Mass. Reg'l editor: Estelle Bond Gurlanick Design consultant: Nancy Wing

AUGUST

_____

_____

_____

_____

_____

_____

_____

_____

_____

_____

_____

_____

_____

_____

_____

_____

_____

Country
DECORATING
Goes
Uptown

PHOTOGRAPHS: BARBARA MARTIN. DESIGN: MARK ABRAMS, THE GUILD HALL. REGIONAL EDITOR: MARY ANNE THOMSON

Sweet honey pine and gingham checks sitting by sleek black leather? Why not! When Alabama-born Mark Abrams planted his country roots in a downtown St. Louis dwelling, a fresh decorating hybrid cropped up.

BY SANDRA S. SORIA

Uptown Country

Designer Mark Abrams coaxes country to grow into a more sophisticated style. Forget rooms stuffed with down-home doodads, Mark represents the new country outlook—one that's leaner, cleaner, and ready to match the simple way we want to live in the '90s.

This designer's home is a study in contrasts. Here, black plays off white, the formal mingles with the friendly, and country charm meets city sophistication. "I like to mix things up a bit," says Mark, his southern lilt further softening that understatement. "Doing the unexpected is a lot more interesting—and fun."

Even though pairing up country and contemporary seems an unlikely design marriage, for Mark it's simply a natural reflection of his own two-sided personality. Born and raised in southern comfort, Mark launched his design career in hard-edged New York City. "I carry my childhood around with me," he says. "I remember Aunt Bessie's beautiful crewel rugs and my grandmother's marble-top table. But later I learned country or traditional pieces have more impact when you give them a contemporary presentation."

This interior designer makes these style opposites attractive, but for many of us, mixing up is hard to do. Unless you use Mark's foolproof-mixer method. "Number one, buy by color," says Mark, now creative director for The Guild Hall, a company specializing in antique and reproduction furniture of all styles.

Black and creamy white are the color ties that bind the room's split personality. From these primary colors, Mark pulls out softer values—white drifts into beige, black fades to gray—to give the spaces eye-soothing flow. Against the neutral backdrop, splashes of color—the russet leather dining chair seats or the red quilt patches—become surprises as welcome as bright blooms in a sea of green.

If scheming for a basic color palette is tip Number One in Mark's book of mix-and-match design, then selecting basic pieces is a close second. "Most of my core pieces are solid in color and clean in line," Mark says. "It's the same idea as a woman who needs the simple black dress as a staple in her wardrobe; I buy the simple black chair because it goes with anything."

Buying basic paves the way for Mark's third tip: "When you start with basic surroundings, you can change the look completely for very little money—just play with fabric and accessories." If he wants to play up the country side of his home's character, he tosses on some floral pillows, brings out a few more quilts, and plunks down a jug of loosely arranged garden flowers. To slick down the style, the quilts and florals hide in the closet when stripes or faux leopard prints come into play. In the winter, deep-toned plaids

Honey pine twinkles against midnight-dark walls.

Bolts of fabric jolt this space to life.

and paisleys warm the scheme.

Getting big impact from low-cost accents makes Mark's style accessible as well as exciting. With $10 worth of paint and a $40 flea-market quilt, his dining room wall (*opposite*) gives a dramatic performance. On the bedroom walls (*left*), fabric takes the spotlight. A couple of bolts of scenic toile de Jouy and a staple gun are the players; Mark simply folded under the raw edges of the fabric, stretched the yardage tight, and then stapled the fabric into place. "I've used this fabric on my walls in three bedrooms now," says Mark. "When I leave I just take a little screwdriver, pull up the staples, roll the fabric, and move on."

No doubt about it, when you want to add drama to a room, you can cast fabric in a range of roles. With Mark as director, even bed linens enter and exit the scene like actors in a play, spicing the setting with a new outlook. "I think you should change your linens like you change your clothes," he says, "to match the season or simply to adjust to your mood." The bed's gray checked spread shows its flip side—crisp white—in the summer months. Come winter, Mark reverses it once more an couples it with a red sheet for a blast of color.

In Mark's home, the point is to lighten up. We're not just talking about less stuff against crisper backdrops. Mark's whole approach to decorating is more relaxed, as carefree as it is clutterfree. It's a point well taken. Keeping it simple means having more fun; you can even change your rooms for the sake of change if you so desire. "I shuffle things around like crazy," Mark says. "If I don't, I get bored."

This designer's enlightened attitude is catchy. The trend in design is to pare down, sacrifice quantity for quality, and simplify, simplify, simplify. What's the big idea? Toss out the excess and you'll make room for what you truly love. Hiding a treasured family piece in a huddle of objects? Clear the way for it to shine on its own.

Above all, decorating by heart means learning to trust your instincts. Think you might like black dining room walls? You never know until you try. After all, what do you have to lose but a few dollars' worth of paint?

TABLE GRACE
Setting the Stage for Elegant Dining

Warm up a dining area with pine furnishings, light, and color. Then, add a snowdrift of lace to the table.

PHOTOGRAPHS: BARBARA MARTIN. DESIGN: MICHAEL HOFFMAN. REGIONAL EDITOR: MARY ANNE THOMSON

Serve up a feast for the eyes whenever you sit down to dinner. Set a savory stage of appetizing colors, generous furnishings, and entertaining accessories that'll keep your guests hoping for another invitation. Begin with a basic backdrop that plays host to everything from a formal sit-down dinner to a casual birthday buffet. No greedy patterns crowd the walls here. Simple stripes and faux-marble wall coverings adapt well to any table-setting theme.

Let your guests drink in the beauty of the room. First, please them with comfortable furnishings: Traditional pine pieces quickly warm a room, inviting everyone to stay awhile. Add fabric personality with chintz chair cushions and a dhurrie rug

Arrange a scene in an open hutch to reflect the table's theme.

that anchors the table grouping. To give yourself storage, display spaces, and a serviceable buffet, settle in a sideboard and a hutch with open shelves nearby. Then, serve everyone delicious scenery. Set a theme for dinner and pull out linens, dishes, lights, and flowers that fit the occasion. Here, dressed-up French country style is played out with white lace, formal dinnerware, and symmetrical lighting. A bit too stilted? Take the edge off formality with springtime flowers arranged casually in a serving bowl. Display down-home dinnerware in the hutch as if you were at home in a thatched-roof cottage.

Finally, satisfy your guests with delightful decorations. Add eye-catching surprises to the setting. Brown paper pigs tied up in purple bows came to this party. And, quite at home in the city, thank you, a rooster crows from the sideboard. ▨

SITTIN' PRETTY
ON THE
PORCH

BY SANDRA SORIA AND WILLIAM L. NOLAN

AH-H-H . . . THERE'S NOTHING LIKE A BREEZY PORCH TO LULL US OUT OF A HECTIC DAY. SURE, ANY OLD HOT-WEATHER SITTING SPOT WITH A RUSTY OLD CHAIR OR TWO IS FINE, BUT CREATE A PEACEFUL ATMOSPHERE—PACKED WITH PERKS—AND YOU HAVE A TRUE STEPS-AWAY RETREAT. LOOKING FOR A SPOT TO KEEP YOUR COOL WHILE THE MERCURY MOUNTS? OUR SITTIN'-PRETTY SAMPLER OFFERS GREAT IDEAS YOU CAN BORROW TO BUILD AND FURNISH A PORCH OF YOUR OWN.

WICKER WONDERLAND

When interior designer Susan VanOrsdel wants to get away from it all, she simply heads for the back door of her Iowa home. There, a shady, screened-in porch waits to soothe her with friendly white wicker and a garden of soft color. The VanOrsdels screened in a section of a deck to create the rain-or-shine retreat, then filled it with vintage furnishings for a comforting, nostalgic aura. Take note of these ideas:

ROLLER BLINDS offer inexpensive wind and sun blockers that will roll up, up, and away when you want an uncluttered view of the outdoors.

WOVEN RUGS are tossed around to add warmth and define conversation areas—and are tossed just as easily into the washing machine when they soil.

CRISP COTTON FABRICS feel as comfortable as a summer sundress. Mix patterns, such as geometrics and florals, for a lively look.

HOUSEPLANTS move to the porch during warm months to blur the distinction between indoors and out—and to recover from the winter blahs.

NATURAL ATTRACTION

Mother Nature helped inspire this backyard porch addition. The homeowners wanted a casual, low-upkeep retreat that blended with the wooded setting, so they paneled the porch with natural-finish Alaskan white cedar and paved the concrete floor with bluestone, a blue-green stone that resembles slate. The screened openings stop a few feet from the floor to keep out dirt and water when it rains. Dark green canvas shades, Adirondack-green wicker furnishings, and floral-print pillows add splashes of color.

Setback restrictions on one side inspired the architect to angle both side walls, creating a bay-front porch. A half-round window in the gable grabs extra light. A large skylight curves over the roof peak, delivering light to the back part of the porch and the adjoining dining room. Tag these features as must-haves for your porch:

LIGHT GRABBERS keep it bright even on cloudy days.

A WHISPER-QUIET CEILING FAN delivers instant relief in muggy weather.

GARDEN-FRESH HUES in the furnishings add a natural flair.

DESIGNER/BUILDER: ROBERT S. WALKER, DESIGN ALTERNATIVES. LANDSCAPE ARCHITECT: CRAIG BERGMAN. PHOTOGRAPHS: JESSIE WALKER ASSOCIATES

LAZY-DAY GETAWAY

When the Franke family moved into their Michigan home, they were full of ideas for improving the porch. Then, they adopted a "let-it-be" philosophy. Says Mary Franke, "We realized we would lose what we loved most—the cottage charm." To gain contemporary comforts without marring the mood, the Frankes freshened with paint and wired their porch for discreet electrical extras (note the tiny suspended speakers that deliver sound without spoiling the space's vintage look). Then, they invited in aged, natural beauties of wicker and pine to serve as storage and seating. Borrow these notions for your porch:

RECESSED FIXTURES light up the night and ceiling fans cool down the day.

DECK ENAMEL covers damaged wood in a hurry, and puts a coat of armor on porch floors. Here, the deep green hue also warms the space.

DOORWAYS to the living room and kitchen direct traffic through the porch and offer easy access to food preparation. With a nod to the garden, lattice-style crosshatching on the doors enhances the outdoor feeling.

A CORNER ON PRIVACY

To get his creative juices flowing, author/columnist Jay Cronley retreats to his favorite getaway: the pavilionlike screened porch he added to his 1940s ranch in Tulsa. Views of the spacious garden offer inspiration; comfy wicker and bamboo chairs put him at his ease. "It's the kind of place," says Jay, "that people search for on vacation and seldom find."

The ceiling reaches for the sky, but the porch is small enough for intimate conversation. French doors offer easy access from the deck and the master bedroom.

The brick pillar in the outside corner houses a phone line and a cable TV outlet, and the roof consists of four large skylights that capture abundant natural light. The floor is simply an extension of the deck—moisture drains right through the closely spaced planks. Take note of this trio of ideas worth adapting:

DECK-STYLE FLOOR provides quick drainage after a downpour.

DOUBLE DOORS aid traffic flow during parties.

BUILT-IN OUTLETS make it easy to bring out the phone and TV.

ARCHITECT: STEVE OLSON, AIA. LANDSCAPE DESIGN: PETER STAMILE. PHOTOGRAPHS: BOB HAWKS. REGIONAL EDITOR: NANCY E. INGRAM

A PLACE IN THE SUN

Don't have a porch to call your own? Any light-filled space can take its place if you furnish it with outdoor appeal. Airy-light furniture and sun-baked accessories bring an earthy outlook to this Seattle sun-room. Here are some ideas you can take home:

THE ALL-WHITE WALLS AND CEILING appear to widen the narrow space and bounce daylight around to brighten the room.

SLEEK MINIBLINDS block out a glaring sun, then disappear when you don't need them.

A WEATHERED CHAIR and curlicued wicker offer cues to outdoor elements.

A WHITEWASHED WOOD FLOOR looks like a deck—or a toasty stretch of sand.

SEPTEMBER

HOME OF THE YEAR

BY WILLIAM L. NOLAN,
DENISE L. CARINGER,
AND ROBERT E. DITTMER

Make that, "Home of the Decade."

We build idea-packed show homes every year to keep you posted on the latest trends in design and products, but this time we outdid ourselves. Even as you stroll up the front walk, our 1990 show house surrounds you with intriguing new products and ideas you can add to your own dream home, whether you build it now or 10 years from now.

Designed by architect Ken Dahlin and built by

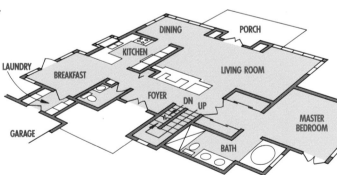

FLOOR PLAN

The main rooms share a 1900s sense of openness while clustering around the hearth—the age-old focus of family life.

The Housing Group in Alpharetta, Georgia, this show house earned rave reviews from builders attending their annual convention in Atlanta. But we knew we had a winner even before we broke ground; Dahlin's design earned the Grand Award in an annual design contest we cosponsor with the American Plywood Association, the American Wood Council, and *Progressive Architecture* and *Builder* magazines.

PHOTOGRAPH: MIKE MORELAND. ILLUSTRATION: MIKE HENRY

A whole new style

The new look we've created for 1990 is so distinctive that we put a label on it: 90s Modern. In part, 90s Modern is a fresh look at what we've always liked about modern—clean lines, flowing space, earthy colors. It also celebrates our ties to the past: wide cornices, tall windows, a cedar shake roof. Working with furnishings from The Lane Company, Inc., *Better Homes and Gardens®* Interior Design Editor Robert Dittmer echoed the architecture by mixing old and new: modern lines cleanly drawn using time-honored wood, wicker, and tile.

The spatial drama climaxes in the living room. Beneath a skylighted vault, the walls form comfortable boundaries, inviting you to curl up by the fire. Soaring spaces deliver drama but can be a bit daunting once you sit down. The remedy: anchor yourself with furnishings, colors, and textures that have visual weight. Here, Lane's leather

SOURCES

Glass table, club chairs, hassock: LANE Table lamp: KOCH AND LOWY. Floor lamps: PAUL HANSON. Floor tile: AMERICAN OLEAN. Heat-circulating fireplace: SUPERIOR

Photographs: Bill Stites. Architect: Ken Dahlin Interior design: Robert E. Dittmer. Builder: The Housing Group. Landscape architect: Matarazzo Design, Inc. Regional editor: Ruth Reiter

HOME OF THE YEAR

armchairs, slick yet substantial, rest atop richly hued kilim rugs. Glowing pools of lamplight lend low-level warmth.

Space to spare

The living room includes two conversation areas, a room-size dining alcove, and generous spillover space in the middle. Open stretches in the furnishings scheme show that you need not worry about filling every inch of floor space. Here, the wide-open spaces behind the fireside area create generous "breathing room," as well as grand access to the French doors

and the terrace beyond them. Bonus: On holidays there's room to serve the whole clan at one sitting.

Corner lounge

Langorous lounges and supple side chairs let you settle back and drink in the dignified serenity of the great-room. We chose lounges here because traditional sofas would have blocked the flow of space and light. And what better choice for a spot that beckons you to settle back and enjoy the view, indoors and out? Whitewashed wooden blinds orchestrate the sun.

SOURCES

Pendent lighting: KOCH AND LOWY Oak flooring: NATIONAL OAK FLOORING ASSOCIATION. Carpet runner: CARPETS BY COLUMBUS, USING "GENESIS" STAIN-RESISTANT FIBER BY AMOCO. Interior corner window: MARVIN WINDOWS Wooden blinds: GRABER. Lounges, armchairs, ladderback chairs, dining table, wrought-iron coffee table: LANE Piano: BALDWIN

Mellow-modern kitchen

Step-saving convenience and streamlined efficiency have always been standard ingredients in the modern kitchen. Our 1990s version improves on the recipe by folding in some mellow softness and extra dollops of sun and space. Gently rounded edges and corners warm up the polished planes on the countertops and flush-front cabinets. Major appliances hug the rear wall, yielding an airier look and more elbowroom in the U-shaped work area.

Good morning, sunshine!

Greenhouse-style bump-outs pump in enough sunshine to revive the grumpiest sleepyhead. Nature's neutrals—charcoal ceramic tile, sandstone Corian countertops, honey-hued built-ins—provide a foil for the sunshine. The clean but homey look derives from vintage-style furnishings sparingly used: a glowing pine table, nostalgic wicker chairs, some fresh-cut sunflowers.

SOURCES

Cabinets: RUTT. Refrigerator, microwave oven: AMANA. Convection oven, cooktop: DACOR. Sink: AMERICAN STANDARD. Floor tile: AMERICAN OLEAN. Cabinet hardware: SUGATSUNE AMERICA. Countertop: DUPONT CORIAN. Breakfast table, wicker chairs: LANE/VENTURE Intercom system: AIPHONE

HOME OF THE YEAR

Morning sun delivers a gentle wake-up call through French doors in the master bedroom. They open to a wraparound deck that hovers in the treetops.

Instead of the usual bedroom basics, our scheme lets you cruise off to Fantasy Island every night. Floating against pale sea-green walls, an exotic bamboo four-poster and island-inspired sheets create the getaway mood.

A tough day? The master bath caresses the kinks with a whirlpool tub at one end, a steam shower at the other, and a storage-lined twin-bowl vanity between.

SOURCES

Glass-top table: LANE. Wicker chair, bamboo chest, bed, and nightstand: LANE/VENTURE. Sheets, pillowcases, comforter: SHERIDAN. Floor lamps: ARTEMIDE. Wooden blinds: GRABER Whirlpool tub, vanity bowls, toilet: AMERICAN STANDARD. Cabinet hardware: SUGATSUNE AMERICA Countertop: DU PONT CORIAN Ceramic tile: AMERICAN OLEAN

HOME OF THE YEAR

The recreation room is really four spaces in one: a TV lounge, an exercise area, a hobby center, and a refreshment bar. No need to dash to the kitchen for sodas during commercial breaks, or miss your favorite soap while doing your daily dozen; the microwave and wine cooler stand ready to serve up snacks and thirst quenchers.

For '90s-style pizzazz, we whitewashed knotty pine, wrapped the TV set with a glass-paneled grid, tiled the floor with sleek, faux-granite vinyl, and energized the action with halogen track lighting. Then we splashed on the fun: bold, jungle-inspired upholstery that brightens the potentially dull, down-under space and says, "Smile! Relax!"

FINISH-LATER SPACE
Expansion space in the walk-out basement houses a multipurpose recreation area, complete with wet bar and half bath. The game room could be a bedroom instead, with its own entrance.

HOBBY CENTER

EXERCISE

SITTING AREA

STORAGE

UTILITY ROOM

UP

GAME ROOM

SOURCES

Vinyl tile: NATIONAL FLOORING COMPANY. Paneling: WESTERN WOOD PRODUCTS ASSOCIATION Home entertainment center: BANG & OLUFSEN. Modular seating: LANE'S PEARSON DIVISION. Track lighting: CAPRI. Microwave oven: AMANA Wine cooler: KEDCO. Countertop and bar sink: DU PONT CORIAN. High-rise faucet: AMERICAN STANDARD. Band saw: BLACK & DECKER. Louvered doors: MORGAN PRODUCTS LTD. Saw and clamps courtesy of K MART

HOME
OF THE
YEAR

'90s design sampler

Thanks to rising construction costs and shrinking lot sizes, bigness for bigness' sake will be out of step with the '90s. Our 90s Modern house offers timely tips for gaining big impact on a modest scale.

1 BOOK NOOK
The study measures a scant 10×10 feet, but painting it mushroom and vaulting the ceiling adds a smidgen of stretch. Open-legged furnishings add comfort without crowding.

2 QUIET VISTA
Marvin's new corner window muffles downstairs noise while preserving dramatic interior views upstairs. Lane/Venture's sleek, white, modular storage pieces melt into the walls.

3 EARTHY CUES
Nature's materials marry the house to its site: roofing from the Red Cedar Shingle and Split Shake Bureau; lap siding from American Plywood Association; treated decks from the Southern Pine Marketing Council; and earth-tone colors by Pratt and Lambert. The

Georgia Water-Wise Council, Matarazzo Design, Inc., and Allgood Outdoors, an Atlanta nursery, created a drought-hardy, water-saving planting scheme.

4 DINING IN?
We rimmed the dining area with high windows and dressed it warmly with sun-bleached oak and pine. Pared-down Lane furnishings give farmhouse shapes a modern spirit.

5 SO HANDY
Space-savvy conveniences equip the work area: American Standard's double-bowl sink, In-Sink-Erator's garbage disposal and hot water dispenser, and KitchenAid's dishwasher.

6 LIGHT SERVINGS
Ready for a coffee break? Lindal's sunspace merges the breakfast room with the terrace.

MIKE MORELAND

HOME OF THE YEAR

1 STRIPE IT BLUE!
Light-handed graphics liven up the family bath: playful blue lines on white porcelain fixtures by American Standard, diamond-patterned tiles by American Olean.

2 TOUCH OF MINK
Our powder room gains presence with mink-colored fixtures from American Standard, wallpaper by FCS Wallcoverings, and a mirrored wall courtesy of the National Association of Mirror Manufacturers.

3 WORK MATES
Chrome pulls from Sugatsune America echo the rounded corners on Rutt's Ellipse cabinet fronts and Corian's Sandstone countertop. A fit-

and-trim trash compactor by KitchenAid merges with the cabinetry.

4 DIGITAL STEAM
Steamist's digital controls turn your shower into a steam bath. The generator fits in the linen closet.

■ HIDDEN HELPERS
Noteworthy products hidden from view include: a built-in central vacuum system by Hoover, a wireless home security system from AT&T, and recessed outdoor lighting by Roberts Step-Lite Systems. The home's shell is insulated with fiber-glass batts from Certainteed Corporation and cloaked below grade with Akzo's plastic-mesh drainage system.

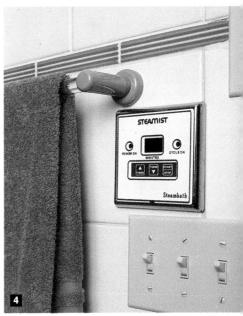

Building a show house takes a lot of hope, stamina, professional expertise, and teamwork. Here are the folks whose creative genius and tireless energies produced our 1990 Innovation House.

(*From left*) Joe Porter, regional marketing manager, American Wood Council; Maryann Olson, project coordinator, American Plywood Association; Michael C. Ray, president, The Housing Group; Rob Bloomquist, project manager, The Housing Group; Ken Dahlin, architect.

(*Left*) William L. Nolan, senior building and remodeling editor, *Better Homes and Gardens;* Robert E. Dittmer, interior design editor, *Better Homes and Gardens.*

(*Left*) Bill Martin, advertising director, The Lane Company, Inc.; Terry Allen, interior designer, the Pearson Company.

ROOM ARRANGING
MADE EASY

BY SANDRA S. SORIA

ONCE UPON A TIME, ROOMS WERE AS PREDICTABLE AS THE I.R.S. IN THE SPRING. YOU ATE IN THE DINING ROOM, PLAYED IN THE FAMILY ROOM, AND RESERVED THE LIVING ROOM FOR COMPANY. TODAY'S OPEN FLOOR PLANS AND DO-IT-ALL GREAT-ROOMS MAKE THOSE OLD ROLES OBSOLETE. WHAT'S NEW: CHOOSING AND ARRANGING FURNITURE TO MAKE ANY SPACE LIVE THE WAY *YOU* NEED IT TO. WANT TO MAKE NEW ARRANGEMENTS AT YOUR PLACE? STUDY THESE ROOMS, THEN GET OUT THE GRAPH PAPER

ROOM ARRANGING DIVIDE AND CONQUER

You won't find an 8-foot sofa here; smaller seaters are easier to arrange in a long, narrow room.

This unit pulls double duty: It entertains on one side of the room, serves meals on the other.

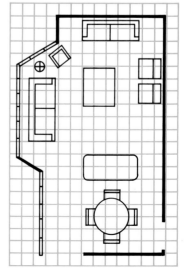

To battle their great-room's tunnellike dimensions, the Young family got strategic; they placed a long, low storage piece crosswise in the space's center, breaking it into two "rooms." In another bold move, they spanned the end wall with posters to visually widen the space.

ROOM ARRANGING RETHINK YOUR SPACES

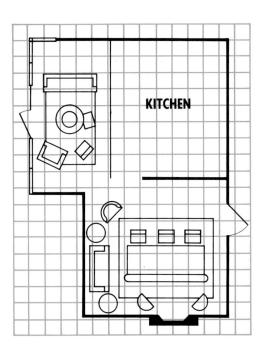

KITCHEN

In this Tulsa ranch house, owner Nancy Ingram tossed aside room labels and arranged the spaces for how her family really lives. At one time, the Ingrams used their modified-L floor plan in the expected way: the area off the kitchen was for dining; the front room for sitting. Then, Nancy realized there had to be a better plan. "Our guests hovered around the dining table to enjoy the sunny space and visit with the cook," she says. "The problem was, the bench was uncomfortable to sit on for long periods of time." So, they traded places—shuffling the cozy seating pieces to the window-lined space and placing the harvest table in front of the hearth. "Now the cook is part of the action before the meal is served," reports Nancy, "and it's wonderful to eat by the fire on chilly evenings."

A crackling fire and access to the kitchen make this former living room an inviting dining spot.

PHOTOGRAPHS: GENE JOHNSON. ILLUSTRATIONS: MIKE HENRY
ARCHITECT: JACK ARNOLD, AIA. REGIONAL EDITOR: NANCY E. INGRAM

Though slated
for dining, this
sunny spot with
a view seemed a
likely place to
entertain or to
simply kick back.

ROOM ARRANGING FLOAT YOUR FURNITURE

Resist the urge to put your backs against the wall. Instead, snuggle pieces together for coziness in a big room.

The curved love seat turns its back on the dining table to form a wall between the two areas.

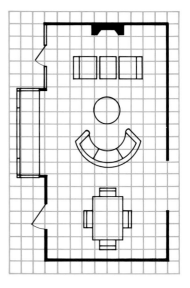

Rather than line walls with furniture in waiting-room fashion, place islands of comfort in the center of a space to create intimacy and better traffic flow. This St. Louis family used the hearth as an anchor, then dropped in a tête-à-tête of sectional seating as a building block for the arrangement. A curvy love seat directs traffic between the room's conversation and dining groups, while it points the way to an exterior door and wet bar.

OCTOBER

'90s Style

THE BEST NEW LOOKS AND WHERE TO GET THEM

What will rooms wear in the '90s? We wondered, too. So we crossed the country for designs to buy, ideas to borrow, and trends to guide you through this decorating decade. For one, we see folks paring down—tossing the clutter to focus on true loves. We're Breaking Tradition, putting classic beauties in stripped-down settings that show off each curve. Even tradition's country cousin, a style we call The Rural Route, leads to quieter schemes that better reflect our simple past. While digging our rooms' roots, we've struck a vein of ethnic energy. Peek at The New Frontier for a wild-west mix of earthy colors and touchable textures. Maybe your soul connects to The Old Country, where softer finishes and fabrics speak with European accents. By following our hearts, we're getting braver along the way. Want a gutsy style? Go to the Hot Tropics, where high-voltage hues spark a bold new look.

BREAKING TRADITION

THE NEW FRONTIER

THE RURAL ROUTE

HOT TROPICS

THE OLD COUNTRY

'90s Style

BREAKING TRADITION

Welcome to the new look of tradition, or is it the new modern? In the '90s, the styles are merging, living happily together under one roof. From *Crate & Barrel,* this grouping inherits classic lines, crisp botanicals, and glowing wood tones from tradition's side of the family. "But this is tradition with a twist," says Lon Habkirk, Crate & Barrel creative director. "We dressed a classic Hepplewhite sofa in a woven cotton fabric to take the stodginess out of it." Besides lightened-up fabrics, a modern heritage shows up in sleek lighting and a spare setting. Like a good marriage, the union brings out each style's best: tradition's warmth takes the cold edge from contemporary's sparse serenity.

Photograph: Steven Hall
Regional editor: Elaine Markoutsas

THE NEW FRONTIER

This wild-west roundup from *The Ralph Lauren Home Collection* whoops and hollers about a new design attitude: We're uncovering cultural roots and celebrating their earthy, downright primitive beauty. As designer Ralph Lauren knows, Americans have long enjoyed a love affair with days gone by. This look expresses the rugged, natural spirit in all of us. Whether rooted in the plains or jungles, ethnic styles boast rich color, rough texture, and handmade charm. Even if you don't want to be back in the saddle again, here's how to give a home soul: Hit the happy trails to furniture stores, flea markets, or the backyard to find objects that speak honestly to you, spark a comforting memory, or invite in nature's unpolished beauty.

Photographs: Judith Watts

'90s Style

THE RURAL ROUTE

Put on a diet since the indulgent '80s, country design has emerged leaner than ever, ready to serve the simpler way of life we crave. American classics, such as these arts-and-crafts and Shaker inspired pieces from *Storehouse*, rise like cream to create the crisp rural look. A bonus? The simple beauties are easy as Mom's apple pie to mix together or blend with what you have. Says Mary Warner, Storehouse furniture buyer: "The beauty of pieces with classic lines is that you can take them to any style of room and they'll feel at home." Here's another fringe benefit: Less clutter means less to buy (and less to dust). The best shopping strategy? Select clean-lined basics, then personalize with a few of your favorite things.

Photographs: Rick Taylor
Regional editor: Ruth L. Reiter

HOT TROPICS

Even once-timid decorators now bravely splash their rooms with living color and stock them with playful furnishings. Forget impressing the neighbors; we're expressing ourselves—and loving it! With sizzling hues and patterns, these hot numbers from *Expressions* take the dare. "Today's shopper doesn't need anyone's stamp of approval," says Expressions president Ronna Griest. "Our homes confidently reflect who we are." For those who wish life were truly a beach, cabana stripes, fun-loving accents, and color-drenched chairs offer island hospitality. A cool white ceramic floor and paneling weathered with paint complete the getaway mood. Ah-h-h-h, you can almost feel the sand between your toes.

Photographs: Jon Jensen

THE OLD COUNTRY

Slavishly replicated and overly decorated schemes are moving over to make room for less tense, more livable style mixes. In the process, we're learning what Europeans have known all along: Charm comes less from what you have than how you use it. This collection from *Lexington* gets its relaxed spirit from back-roads Europe. "Europeans love a house that looks lived in," says the line's designer, Lynn Hollyn. "If decoration is too perfect or untouchable, the life vanishes from a room." The mixture of gently painted wood finishes and delicate fabric patterns gives this room an instantly evolved look; then, the simple background gives it quiet country charm. BH&G

Photograph: Bill Ellis
Regional editor: Katherine Wiglesworth

ADDING UP

2ND-STORY ADDITIONS

BY TOM JACKSON

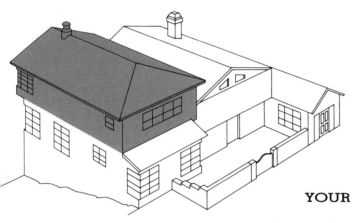

YOU LIKE YOUR NEIGHBOR-HOOD, THE SCHOOLS AND FRIENDS, AND YOU WANT TO STAY PUT. BUT YOUR HOME IS ABOUT TO BURST AT THE SEAMS, AND YOUR LOT LEAVES NO ROOM TO ADD ON.

WHAT DO YOU DO? TRY ADDING UP WITH A SECOND-STORY ADDITION.

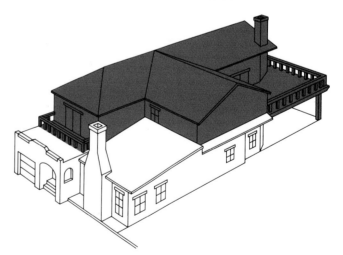

YOU CAN DOUBLE YOUR SQUARE FOOTAGE, OR ADD JUST ENOUGH TO CREATE A COZY PARENTS' HIDEAWAY. EITHER WAY, YOU GET THE ELBOW-ROOM YOU NEED IN THE NEIGHBORHOOD YOU'VE GROWN ACCUSTOMED TO.

HERE ARE THREE ADDITIONS THAT TAKE THE HIGH GROUND: A SPANISH STYLE, A MODERN HOME, AND A CLASSIC RANCH.

ILLUSTRATIONS BY MIKE HENRY

ADDING UP

Wraparound windows point your gaze toward the best views, and the solid walls screen out the neighbors.

Sunshine from the skylight illuminates the stairwell. The open plan helps pull light into the rear of the master suite and the first floor below.

SIMPLY MODERN
Parents create a nest with treetop views

Nobody but the birds and squirrels knew the views were so spectacular until the family added this 550-sq.-ft. master suite to their home.

Capturing the views without losing privacy on this narrow lot required wraparound windows in the front pointed toward the views and a solid wall that screens out the neighbors on the sides.

The curve of the stairwell opening lends a soft touch to the linear design.

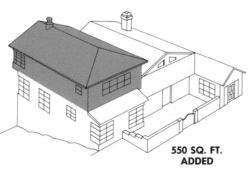

550 SQ. FT. ADDED

ARCHITECT: WILLIAM GLASS ASSOCIATES. PHOTOGRAPHS: JAY GRAHAM. REGIONAL EDITOR: HELEN HEITKAMP

Eliminating windows on the sides preserved the privacy in this master suite addition.

Skylights above the stairwell deliver additional light. Viewed from the first floor, this skylight creates a delightfully sunny glow in the stairwell.

Curves in the stairwell opening, baluster, and handrail balance the straight-line geometry of the rest of the room. The circular form that hides the flue above the fireplace also imparts flowing, sculptural qualities.

Years before this remodeling, the owner had beefed up the foundation in anticipation of someday adding the second story. Space for the stairwell was taken from one end of a downstairs bedroom.

PUEBLO POP-UP

New bedrooms and baths elevate the family out of cramped quarters.

Liberation for the lower floor of this once tiny, two-bedroom, 1,000-sq.-ft. home came with the addition of three bedrooms upstairs. Once the sleeping quarters went skyward, the downstairs was allowed to spread out, creating spacious living areas that include a new dining room, an enlarged kitchen, and a bigger living and family room. The new arrangement clearly separates public and private spaces in the home, al-

BEFORE

lowing sleepers to snooze upstairs without being disturbed by the bustle of busier rooms.

Upstairs, the family gained a master suite, two bedrooms and a bath for the kids, and a laundry room. The parents have privacy, and there are enough bathrooms so that the family isn't forced to shower in shifts. The master bedroom works as a parents' retreat, with a desk, bookshelves, a television and entertainment center, and a fireplace. Outside the double French doors, a wraparound balcony provides a fresh-air retreat and a private view of the backyard.

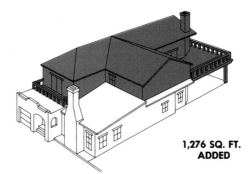

1,276 SQ. FT.
ADDED

From lowbrow to high style, a second-story addition lifted this comfortable, spacious home out of a tiny, boxlike dwelling.

ADDING UP

The master bedroom covers all the angles, with a fireplace, a balcony, and media-wall storage.

Painted white, the trim details and ceiling raise your line of sight and help make a narrow space feel larger.

TOP-DRAWER TRADITION

Raising the ranch with a master suite

Even the low-slung profile of a ranch-style home can sit tall in the saddle with a well-designed upstairs addition.

With five growing children squeezed into this single-story home, the parents decided to perch their nest up top, thus freeing an extra bedroom for the older kids. Now, whenever slumber parties produce a platoon of noisy kids, the parents can escape upstairs.

The gable on the front end of the house encloses a long bedroom and sit-

When properly proportioned, an upstairs addition perches perfectly, even on a ground-hugging ranch-style home.

ting area. The vaulted ceiling and white painted woodwork break up the long narrow space with eye-catching architectural elements. A window seat at one end houses quilts and extra bedding. Shelves on each side of the window seat hold collectibles that give the room a comfortable, personal touch. The wing that parallels the main roofline contains a spacious bath.

The addition went up quickly. The contractor built the new subfloor on top of existing ceiling joists, allowing the family to remain in the home during the remodeling. BH&G

Parents can put themselves on top of the fray by adding up with a low-slung but spacious bath and bedroom combination.

1,000 SQ. FT. ADDED

By Sandra S. Soria

It happens to the best of us. We're in a new city, a great flea market, a foreign land (that we know we'll never see again), when there it is—an object of desire. "What am I going to do with another ... (fill the blank)," you ask, weakening. "It could make a great gift, or fill the blank speck on my shelves." And so, for altruistic reasons, you adopt the forlorn item and lovingly tote it home.

A COLLECTOR'S
PASSION
HOW TO LIVE WITH THE THINGS YOU LOVE

A passion for collecting is tough to resist. And why should you? Adorning rooms with things you adore turns a house into a home, builds its character. Still, as with anything that makes life enjoyable, there's danger in excess. Who wants to live amid a clamor of clutter? Rest easy, here's how to live peaceably with the things you love.

Collector Susan Lipman (*left*) has planned carefully so there's always room in her Chicago home for one more "friend." Wall-to-wall shelves, a host of display cases, and scattered tabletops all stand ready to shelter her latest adoptees. The hardworking furnishings make order out of collectible chaos, and put Susan's loves (and life) proudly on parade. "I'm surrounded by things I've picked up that mean a lot to me," says Susan, who is executive director of Chamber Music Chicago. "They comfort me, and give my home a warm feeling."

Furnished with things she's found along the way in travels—including African masks, a Mexican sofa, and Indonesian textiles—Susan's home is a cross-cultural affair. Despite their disparate origins, the adopted objects blend easily into one big happy family. The ties that bind? Common character traits, such as earthy colors, rough and ready textures, and ethnic energy. Mostly, though, these collections are bound by the curator's heartstrings. "I don't follow strict design rules," says Susan. "There's an overall sense of what belongs. I put what I like together, and, voilà, it works for me."

"MY THINGS COMFORT ME, WARM MY HOME."

Susan Lipman has been raking in books since age 9, when she joined book clubs under assumed names to get more freebies.

More than a roundup of things, the best collections compose a one-of-a-kind collage that reveals our lives and loves. Susan's collections greet her warmly, like old friends. "When I step into this room after work each night," she says, "I smile."

There's nothing formal about this dining room. Friendly gatherings, from mismatched chairs to well-thumbed cookbooks, welcome guests with open charms. The relaxed attitude they share helps the elements get along visually.

To personalize a place, display heartfelt interests like an open book. Nothing expresses you like books and art—two loves that line Susan's walls.

HOW TO LIVE WITH COLLECTIONS

● **Choose items that say something to you—or about you.** If you limit displays to things you love, chances are that even unlikely mixes will make a match.

● **Group items for impact.** Scattered objects get lost in space; instead, huddle your loved ones on a table, a shelf, or in a corner for visual strength in numbers.

● **Unify a gathering with items similar in mood, style, or color.** Susan's garden of earthy delights is bound by natural hues and textures.

● **Keep backgrounds simple,** like a gallery, to prevent eye overload. White walls and neutral floors "air out" a lot of objects, giving them room to breathe on their own.

● **Arrange eye-pleasing displays.** In a grouping, place taller objects in back, smaller objects in front, then stagger heights slightly in between. Draw attention to mini items by framing them with a tray or fabric.

● **Know when to stop.** Collections become clutter when your eye can't pick out any one object to rest on.

The best collections have connections, not only to our memories, but to the way we live now. The objects of Susan's affections aren't touch-me-nots, trapped forever behind glass. Her pieces move about freely for an interesting change of place, or they leap into action. For instance, the Spanish *paella* bowls now resting on the dining table (*left*) serve snacks when guests arrive.

Want to start a collection or show what you have to its advantage? Think about your life's little pleasures—closeted keepsakes to modern-day romances—and compose them into a family portrait. Use your tables, walls, and home as the perfect frame. [BH&G]

SUPER-SLEEK MASTER BATH
Soothing luxury, quiet style

This master bath helps launch a two-career couple into their busy workdays. The soothing decor and the whirlpool tub take the stress out at day's end, too.

Topping a two-story addition with this 9×12-foot bathroom netted the Steinbergs some amenities they never had before, including a whirlpool bath and double vanity. Two medicine cabinets, one above each sink, merge with the mirrored wall above the vanity. A niche under the makeup counter houses a comfortable stool. The countertop is solid marble.

Setting the tub, the steps leading to it, and the floor tiles on a diagonal provides visual relief in a room dominated by rectangles. Angling the tub also yielded handy ledges in the corners of the tub platform. For continuity, the high windows on two outside walls are matched by mirrors of the same size over the doorway. The casement window near the tub opens for ventilation. The Steinbergs converted the old bathroom on the second floor into a walk-in closet. In the added space on the first floor, below the new master bath, they built two smaller bathrooms. The total cost of remodeling was $65,000. 📷

A glass door partially closes off the toilet stall for privacy, at right.

Items from the couple's contemporary art collection bring cheer to the room.

Two steps lead from the bedroom (behind louvered doors, left) up to the bathroom.

NOVEMBER

fINISHING TOUCHES

Accessories That

Make Your

House a Home

BEFORE

*Y*our sofa is in place,

the chair looks inviting,

and the lamp is plugged

in. Still, something's missing. Could it be that you stopped decorating too soon?

Consider the extra touches that fill in a room's blanks with instant personality.

By Robert E. Dittmer, Rebecca Jerdee, and Sandra S. Soria

PHOTOGRAPHS: PERRY STRUSE

*L*earn to master the mix. The urns did a beautiful job of visually linking mirror to bureau, but they looked lonely. As leaves add lushness to a landscape, this tablescape improved when filled in with objects. Remember, opposites attract attention: pair fat (urns) with skinny (topiaries), rough (terra-cotta) with smooth (glass), and large (leafy plant) with small (lovable Teddy).

BEFORE

*C*ultivate warmth; plant the right accessories. It took just a few timeworn treasures to fire up this lukewarm scheme. Ethnic textiles spark it with color

BEFORE

and texture, then a curvy armchair adds the glow of polished wood. Golden lamplight and luscious, leafy plants turn up the heat even further. Finally, don't forget wellstocked bookcases. Your first-grade teacher was right: Books build character.

FINISHING
TOUCHES

BEFORE

PERRY STRUSE

*g*ather objects of affection in a close-knit group. Inherited family furnishings, such as the table and rocker shown here, join hands with a friendly screen made from antique doors. Together, they corner some privacy in a room. Touch up your own similar arrangement with a pair of antique prints, tabletop treats (note the pretty peach potpourri and majolica), and an antique tapestry pillow.

Buying information, page 76.

*g*o to great panes with fabrics. What a difference a decorating day makes: Yesterday this bare-bones window seat invited no sitters. Today, with a light-filtering fabric shade, a lyrical valance, and soft, cushioned seating, it offers a cozy nook for reading and a side table for tea and trinkets.

BEFORE

PHOTOGRAPHS: JON JENSEN. DESIGN: JOHN AND ANITA VARME

172

FINISHING
TOUCHES

*g*ive barren walls gallery glory. You may have the antidote for ho-hum walls hiding in albums or scattered about in old frames, unnoticed. Invite cherished family photos to a reunion, turning that blah spot into one that evokes a smile. For impact, outline loved ones with crisp, new frames.

*e*ntertain new ideas for the table. Framed family scenes set aglow by twinkling tree lights and crystal coax a meal's mood down memory lane. Place your photos in the round so that no guest stares at a frame back.

PHOTOGRAPHS: PERRY STRUSE

175

BEFORE

*t*ransform lazy corners into hard workers. *Before, this corner looked good enough, but didn't pull its own weight in a small living room. Accessories that serve a duty while they add beauty saved the day. Slip in a writing table, an easy armchair, and well-placed cushions, for instance, and this underdeveloped area is at your service. If you don't have a ready bench to build around, create one fast with modular storage pieces or a vintage trunk.*

FINISHING
TOUCHES

PHOTOGRAPHS: GENE JOHNSON. REGIONAL EDITOR: NANCY E. INGRAM

i *mprove your bedside manner. Is the same old nightstand with lamp putting your bedroom's style to sleep? Give it a wake-up call by corraling collectibles into a still life that says something about your real life. This rowdy roundup whoops it up*

about the owner's passion for western art. Surprise! A chair moves in as a bedside table. If you're letting a piece's expected function rein in your creativity, shuffle your stuff and have some fun.

FINISHING
TOUCHES

*M*ake an entrance with welcome-home style. Instead of hanging about as doors, these latticed bifolds step in as screens to separate the entrance from the rest of the room. For a light-and-airy entry, paint all of the friendly furnishings with white semigloss paint. Then, treat the wall to flat pastels and a soft farewell message.

BEFORE

*C*ollections just want to have fun. So, let them out of their boxes or tight, little shelf arrangements. Here, a multisize collection of chairs broke free from their bound-

aries to climb walls, perch on frames, create tabletop scenes (note how they were given a wider "stage"), and, in general, to enjoy more attention from passersby. If your collection is still under the bed, pull it out and get it back in the high life again.

COLLECTING SPACE DIVIDENDS

▲ **Out of thin air, this attic landing becomes an inviting hideaway with the addition of only three pieces of furniture.**

◄ **Books say a lot about you. Pull treasured tomes out of their attic boxes for shelf life in a hall.**

Take stock of your inactive hallways and stairwells. For a relatively low investment of decorating time and money, you can get a higher return on living space. Come up to the attic of this San Francisco home to see how one family managed it.

The hidden space dividends were at the top of this house, where the staircase ended in a squarish foyer. The foyer skinnied out around the corner in a narrow passage to the back bedroom. Look familiar? Take these steps to get your share of surplus living:

Raise your sites. Consider installing an operable sky window. Not only will it visually lift the space, but you can open it to let stale air out and fresh air in. Here, it sheds natural light on the space under the roof, cheering it up and making the absence of windows unnoticeable.

Whiten and brighten. Where natural light leaves off, paint picks up. Beneath these eaves, dark spaces are lightened with crisp white paint. Because it's light, white paint visually opens up a cramped room, making it seem larger than it really is. To the side of the stairs, a sunshine color subs for nature's own, lightening and brightening the interior.

Fill under-eaves space. Strategic furniture placement helps you cash in on bonus space that's just waiting around the next corner. To make every inch count, place a sofa along the room's lowest wall. This once-wasted space not only performs a vital function as a cozy hideaway, it does double duty as guest quarters. The sofa is a sleeper, whose bedding is cached away inside the coffee table until needed.

Line walls with shelves. Where furniture won't fit, books will. Lined with shelves, this narrow hallway becomes a bountiful backdrop as well as a library within fingertip reach. ▧

DECEMBER

Four-year-old Adrienne is all giggles and smiles when she finds a tiny treasure that Santa left under the tree. She's seated on a chair which was painted by her mom, Gig Schussler, to echo the French Quimper pottery the family collects.

Christmas
FROM THE OLD WORLD

SOMETHING OLD, SOMETHING NEW, *something yellow, something blue. Whether it's the materials used in building their home or the brightly colored, country-French pottery they admire, this young family mixes it all with style and an old-world feeling. They have gathered up the things—and people—they cherish most to create a home filled with love.*

BY JILANN SEVERSON

A Treetop Angel Doll overlooks a pine stuffed with baby's-breath and entwined with grapevine. Crocheted baskets and painted wooden grapes reflect the family's European roots. Embroidered Faience Pillows patterned after Gig's Quimper pottery collection and Sheep Dolls stitched just for Adrienne are surefire favorites for Christmas morn.

A FEELING OF EUROPE LINGERS IN THE HOME

of Gig and Tim Schussler. They're masters at blending, from their European roots and their love of old and new to the paints they mottled on their walls. In their living room, a new cross-stitch sampler where angels proclaim goodwill is bordered in French fabric, and folkish Dutch tiles frame the fireplace. Echoing the simple charm, American rag rugs cover the floors, a garden bench mingles with delicate wicker, and a quilt drapes the modern sofa. Even more impressive: they did it all themselves.

PHOTOGRAPHS: WILLIAM STITES. DESIGN CREDITS, SEE PAGE 151

Adrienne, Tim, and Gig Schussler

185

Christmas
FROM THE OLD WORLD

"EVERYONE TOLD US *it would take forever—and it has!" laughs Gig when she tells about building their house "from the ground up." Tim, a carpenter, incorporated old stained-glass windows with functional new ones in several rooms. Gig, who learned furniture painting from her mother, experimented to find the perfect aged finish she wanted for the walls. Amid all the skill and talent displayed in their home, two standouts are evident: the colorful Quimper (cam PEAR) pottery they collect and Adrienne, their 4-year-old daughter.*

Christmas
FROM THE OLD WORLD

THE SHOP *Gig owns with her parents, Marie and Victor, is also filled with Quimper, colorful pottery painted with old-world figures and flowers. And Adrienne loves it just as much as her parents do.*

"I think Adrienne's first word was Quimper," jokes Tim. He's not far from the truth. When she helps set the table, everyone gets a folkish plate picked just for them. And if her morning snack isn't in a Quimper bowl, she'll let you know.

To make Gig's fresh-fruit and greens centerpiece, cut a piece of plywood to the desired size for your table. Randomly pound nails completely through the wood; cover the board with an assortment of greens. Gently push fresh fruits onto the nails, placing the larger fruits toward the center and tapering to smaller fruits.

SHRIEKS OF LAUGHTER ring through the house when Adrienne sees her grandparents drive up. They're her best buddies. In fact, family is so important to them all that they have turned Christmas into a two-day celebration. Visits to both families mean lots of playful cousins for Adrienne to enjoy.

"We work so hard during the holidays that we like to stretch it out," explains Gig.

Paper Dress-Up Dolls (*below*) and their wardrobes made of papers and trims pose on Gig's painted cupboard. Gig painted the tiny chair to match her Quimper dishes several years ago.

INDEX